Art, Bake and Craft with your Child

Claire H Robinson

For Catherine and George, my wonderful children

"This is the first book I have published. I love making crafts, or baking with my children. It's quality time, where the world stops for half an hour or so and we become engrossed in a little project. I wanted to include activities that I did as a little girl, as well as ones that have been inspired by traditional holidays and festivals throughout the seasons of the year. I hope you enjoy reading my book and doing the activities with your children. Have fun!"

First published in Great Britain in 2013 by Claire H Robinson

ISBN: 978-0-9574809-0-2

A CIP catalogue record for this book is available from the British library

Printed and bound by Lightning Source

NOTES

Children should be supervised at all times. Activities marked "Adult only" are to be carried out only by a responsible adult.

Ovens should be preheated to the specified temperature. The temperature may have to be adjusted for fan-assisted ovens.

Some of the baking activities in this book, may contain foods with nut derivatives. Nuts and peanuts can cause allergic reactions, which are sometimes severe. Pregnant or breast-feeding women, children or the elderly may be particularly vulnerable to foods containing peanuts.

Always supervise your child when they are eating foods that are choking hazards, such as pieces of raw vegetables, fruits or salads.

While the advice and information in this book are believed to be accurate, neither the author nor the publisher can accept any legal responsibility for any illness or accident sustained whilst following the advice or instructions in this book.

Contents

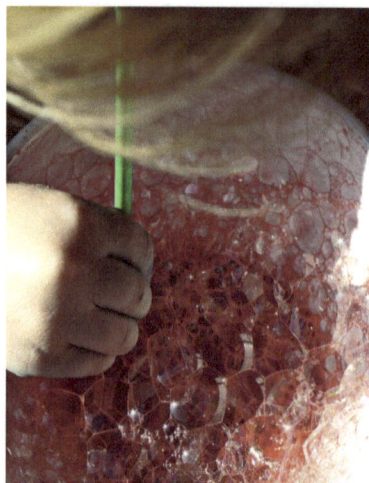

Introduction

About this book

This book contains lots of activities to do with children who love to make and bake. It is aimed at children between the ages of 3 and 10.

The activities will provide hours of fun and enjoyment for you and your child. Once your child has mastered a skill, you will be amazed how quickly they will then be able to carry out some of the projects on their own.

The 52 activities are divided into the four seasons of the year: Spring, Summer, Autumn, and Winter.

It is fascinating to see young animals born in Spring time, and then enjoy recreating collage lambs and chicks. It is wonderful to see beautiful flowers in Summer time, and use their fallen petals to make sweet perfume. It is lovely to go out on a crisp, Autumnal morning and find different coloured and shaped leaves for printing. It is exciting to prepare cotton wool snowmen in the Winter, and then build a real one outside.

Each project has step-by-step instructions, and accompanying photographs.

On each page there is a list of "Associated Activities", which link to the project. These vary from talking points and extra crafts, to games and dance ideas.

"Ideas for Older Children" provide suggestions about how the activity could be extended as your child becomes more proficient.

All of the activities in this book can help your child to reach developmental milestones, and give your child a sense of accomplishment, which is fantastic for their self esteem. The activities will help to develop their fine motor skills, which involve their hand, finger, and wrist action. These can be developed through activities such as cutting, sticking, colouring, peeling, rolling and chopping. Simple mathematics could be introducing when counting, adding and subtracting ingredients or objects. Talking to your child about achieving a balanced diet when carrying out the food based activities, will help them to understand the importance of good nutrition.

The display box marked as "Great for" is a list of the additional skills which your child is developing through doing each activity. Interests in plants and animals, or learning about traditions related to Christmas, Easter and Pancake Day, for example, can be developed.

I have carried out all the activities with my three-year-old daughter, who gets so excited when we get our craft box out, or when we put on our aprons to do some baking together.

Materials

The material used in this book can be bought from craft or baking shops, but to save money try and recycle as much as possible. Re-use old boxes, tinfoil, and ribbons from gift-wrapping. Many of the materials can be used for several projects.

You could keep the art and craft materials and tools in a box, which your child will enjoy decorating with you. The baking materials could be stored separately in the kitchen on their own shelf, along with scales which will be needed to weigh out ingredients for the baking activities, and a large mixing bowl.

Several of the activities involve going out for walks or out into the garden, looking for different materials. Children love being outdoors, and looking for items is just as much as fun as making things with them. Visit the park or local wood to find a pinecone for the bird feeder, or go to the seaside to find shells for a necklace.

Workspace

When doing these activities with young children, there will inevitably be some mess. To keep things to a minimum, put a large wipe-proof mat over the floor or table where you will be working with your child, and put the materials in suitably sized bowls.

Cover their clothes with a wipe-proof apron or old shirt, to protect them from getting covered in paint, glue or baking ingredients. It is a good idea to keep a bowl of warm soapy water nearby, so that you can wash your child's hands in between steps.

It is very important that workspaces and utensils are clean when preparing food. Encourage your child to wipe up any spillages with a clean cloth as they go along.

Your child may enjoy helping with the washing up after you have done some baking. Make sure you protect the floor first though as a lot of the water in the sink may end up there. Show your child how to splash the water to make bubbles. Pass them a small sponge and the dishes, and ask them to put the clean items on the draining board when they have finished. It might be nice to make up a song that you can sing together while you wash up.

Tidying up together is all part of the fun!

Keeping safe

The activities where the adult must be particularly responsible, are marked *"Adult only"* and are highlighted in italics.

A lot of the activities involve cutting things with scissors. If your child can use scissors, make sure they are child-safety ones. There will be activities, however, where you may need to use your own sharp scissors or knife. Keep all sharp blades or tools out of reach of your child.

A drill is needed to make holes in the shells for the necklace and watering can lid. Drills are dangerous and should only be handled by adults.

Baking of teddy bear biscuits, flapjack, Halloween pizza, fairy cakes and mince pies is done in an oven. Pans are used in boiling eggs for the decorated Easter eggs, melting chocolate for the chocolate Easter nests and heart shaped chocolate crispies, and for frying the pancakes. Care must be taken to keep your child well way from hot surfaces, and the parts of these activities where an oven or pan is used should be only be carried out by a responsible adult. Always use oven gloves to remove things from ovens. To create the fruit smoothies, the adult should use the blender. Fruits and vegetables should always be washed.

When doing the food based activities, make sure that your child or anyone that you are preparing food for, doesn't have an allergy to anything you are using.

Germs are spread easily from our hands. Always wash hands thoroughly with soap and warm water before cooking, after touching raw food, going to the toilet or after touching the bin.

Make it fun

The idea of the book is to sit with your child, and do the projects together, until he or she is independent enough to carry them out on their own.

Go shopping with your child to choose the ingredients or craft bits that you will need to carry out the activities. They will enjoy putting them in the basket and then paying for them. Then sit down together and make sure that you have all the materials and tools to hand before you sit down together.

Give yourselves plenty of time to carry out the projects, so that you can give your child your full attention. If they are tired, or not in the mood, leave it for another time. It is important that you both enjoy yourselves. Praise and encourage your child lots. Remember that whatever they create will be beautiful. It's about having fun, and spending quality time together.

Spring

Spring is the first season of the year. Many animals and birds are born, and plants begin to grow.

The weather can be changeable with sunshine, showers and wind. If it's a sunny day use the binoculars to look at flowers and insects in the garden. Make and fly the kite on a windy day. A showery day is perfect to be indoors planting Cress Heads or making a scrapbook about your garden.

Spring covers the months of March, April and May. Decorate eggs, make Chocolate Easter nests or hop about the garden wearing bunny ears to celebrate Easter, which falls during Spring.

Cress Head

This activity is great for introducing your child to gardening, as they will enjoy sowing the seeds and watching them grow. Cress seeds are fantastic, as they grow quickly, and you don't need to use soil.

What you will need:

Hardboiled egg
Spoon
Felt tips or paints
Kitchen roll
Cotton wool
Water
Cress seeds
A bright windowsill

Associated activities:

Cook

Make an egg and cress sandwich. Cut the cress off the top of the cress head, and wash. Mash a hardboiled egg, with the cress and a dollop of mayonnaise. Put your filling in between two slices of bread, and enjoy!

Plant

Growing vegetables with children is more likely to encourage them to eat more vegetables too! Ask your child to pick the seeds, and together plant, care for, and harvest your vegetable plant. Easy to grow vegetables are tomatoes, peppers, carrots and lettuce.

Create your child's name in the garden using cress seeds. With a stick write your child's name in a patch of soil. Cover each letter with seeds. Remind your child to water the patch of soil each day using a watering can, and watch their name grow.

Great for:

exploring nature

learning about plants and seeds

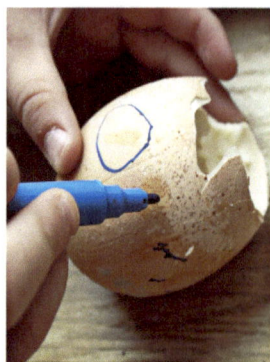

1 *Adult only: Hard-boil an egg.* When cooled, take the top off gently. Scoop out the inside of the egg.

2 Draw a face on the egg shell using felt tips or paints.

3 Wet some kitchen roll, and place at the bottom of the egg shell. Then wet some cotton wool and place on top of the kitchen roll.

4 Sprinkle cress seeds on top of the cotton wool, and press down. Put your Cress Head onto a bright windowsill, and keep checking how it's growing.

Ideas for older children:

Use different materials to add facial features. Make arms and legs for the Cress Head.

Binoculars

Children will love looking through these binoculars to explore the world. Encourage them to go out into the garden and see which birds or insects they can find.

What you will need:

Kitchen roll tube
Scissors
Shiny paper
Glue
Stickers and ribbon
Pencil
String

Associated activities:

Binocular games

Practice using the binoculars with a scanning method. Scan for the birds with your eyes. When you find a bird, lift your binoculars to your eyes without moving your head.

Look through the binoculars, and find things that are green. Count how many things you found. Repeat with different colours.

Draw a picture of a leaf, flower, stick, worm, ladybird etc on a piece of paper. Go into the garden, and search for them there, using the binoculars.

Go on a scavenger hunt. With a list showing photos or pictures of things to find, see who can find all the items the fastest. This game can be played indoors or outdoors. The winner could get a small prize.

1 Cut a kitchen roll tube in half, and decorate the two rolls with shiny paper.

2 Glue the two rolls together.

3 Decorate the rolls with stickers, and ribbon.

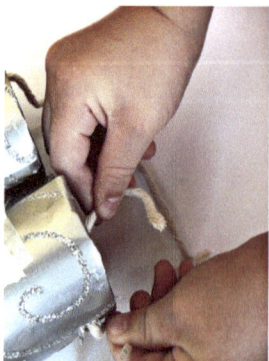

4 Pierce the top of each roll with a pencil, and thread string through the holes. Tie a knot at the back.

Great for:

discovering new things

exploring nature

Ideas for older children:

Make "lenses" for the binoculars. Place a circle of plastic wrap over each hole of the rolls. Secure with an elastic band. Experiment using different coloured plastic wrap to see the world through a variety of colours.

Pancakes

Most children enjoy the tradition of eating pancakes on Pancake Day. Make this simple pancake recipe with your child, who will enjoy mixing the ingredients in the bowl, and watching you cook and flip the pancakes in the air.

What you will need:

For 8 small pancakes:
120g (4oz) plain flour
Pinch of salt
300ml milk
1 egg, beaten
Small knob of butter, melted
Large mixing bowl
Wooden spoon
Whisk
Frying pan
Oil
Accompaniments

Associated activities:

Chat
Explain how Pancake Day, (also known as Shrove Tuesday) is traditionally the last chance to indulge, before giving things up for Lent.

Craft and play
Make a frying pan by taping a lollipop stick to a paper plate. Cut out a pancake shape from heavy cardboard and paint it yellow.

Put the pancake shape in the crafted frying pan. The aim is to throw it up and down, trying to catch the pancake in the pan.

Have a pancake race. Whoever makes it to the finish line first tossing their pancake along the way, wins. However if the pancake is dropped, it's back to the starting line!

Great for:

learning about Pancake Day traditions

learning about kitchen hygiene and safety

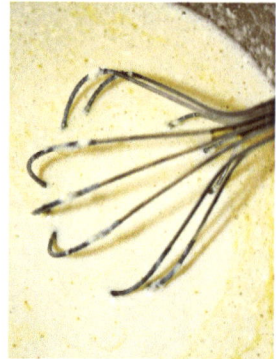

1 Sieve the flour into a large mixing bowl. Add the salt. Make a well in the middle, and fold in the egg and milk.

2 Give the mixture a good whisk, until it is smooth. Add the melted butter.

3 *Adult only: Heat a very small amount of oil in a non-stick pan. Spoon in 4 tablespoons of the pancake mixture. Cook, flip the pancake over, and cook the other side.*

4 Traditionally lemon juice and sugar is added to a pancake when eating. However experiment with adding different flavours to your pancake.

Ideas for older children:

Talk through the instructions of how to make the pancake. Take photos of each step by step stage, mix them up, and ask your child to reorder them.

Potato printing

A great activity for children of all ages. Making a pattern using the potato shape can make wonderful wrapping paper for special presents.

What you will need:

Potato
Child's knife
Shape cutter
Paints
Paper

Associated activities:

Sing

Make a fist shape and turn it sideways, and place on a flat surface. Put your fist on top of your child's. Repeat for each line of the song. Sing "One potato, two potato, three potato, four. Five potato, six potato, seven potato, more. Whoever says "more", removes their hand and starts the song again.

Play

Play Hot Potato with several children. Ask the children to sit in a circle, and pass a ball clockwise around the circle. Ask them to sing "Hot Potato, Hot Potato, Hot Potato Hot, Hot Potato, Hot Potato, Hot Potato Stop!". Whoever has the ball (Hot Potato) when the word "Stop" is sung, is out. Keep playing until one child is left.

1 Cut the potato in half. Choose the shape that you want to make.

2 Draw the shape onto the potato. Then cut around it, so that the shape is raised.

3 Dip the potato shape into the paint, so that the shaped end is completely covered.

4 Press down on the paper with your painted potato shape.

Great for:

developing printing techniques

developing colour and shape awareness

experimenting with patterns

Ideas for older children:

Use different fruit and vegetables such as apples or carrots to make the shapes. Which fruit or vegetable makes the best pattern?

Kite

Flying a kite on a windy day is great fun.
Assemble this easy-to-make kite with your child, and enjoy hours of fun flying it!

What you will need:

Two sticks, one long, one short
Card
Scissors
Paints and brushes or crayons
Tape
String
Tissue paper
A windy day!!

Associated activities:

Chat

Talk about kites and flying them. Ask the children how kites stay in the air. Discuss the wind. Very strong winds and insufficient winds can both create problems when flying a kite. The way the trees are moving can usually give an idea of the strength and direction of the wind. Show your child pictures of kites in books or on the internet. Talk about the different shapes they are made up of, diamond, triangles etc.

Dance

Pretend to be a kite. Use swirling motions with hands. Bend and jump with the body. Pull a scarf through the air like the kite tail.

Game

Talk about how strong the wind is. On a windy day, bring items outside, such as a leaf, paper, stick, stone etc. to see how much the wind blows heavy and light objects.

1 Find two light wooden sticks, one longer than the other, and tape them together to form a cross shape.

2 Cut a diamond shape out of card, the same length and width as the cross. Decorate the card with paints or crayons.

3 Attach the card to the sticks, using tape. Tape a length of string onto the bottom of the card.

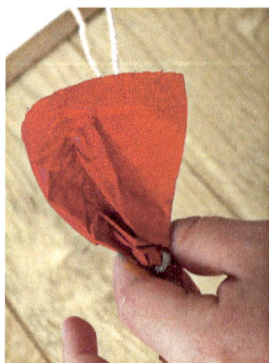

4 Tie bits of tissue paper along the length of the string.

Great for:

learning about different weather types

increasing knowledge of shapes

Ideas for older children:

Use other materials to make your the kite, such as fabric. Discuss which materials help the kite to fly better.

Bird mobile

Mobiles are hanging sculptures which look fantastic adorned with your child's work.
Suspend this bird mobile in your child's room with a hook or push pin.

What you will need:

Card
Scissors
Paints and brushes
Textured or patterned
materials, such as feathers
Googly eyes
Glue
Two sticks
String
Pencil

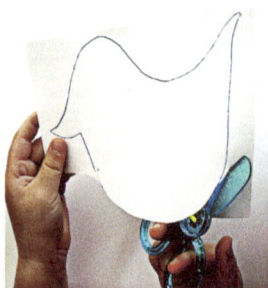

Associated activities:

Chat

Place binoculars and bird books next to the window so that your child can view real birds, and find them in the book. Talk about their colours, and other characteristics.

Game

Cut out a lot of pictures of different birds. Which have you seen? Blue Tits, Sparrows, Blackbirds, Goldfinches and Robins are amongst the commonest British birds.

Craft

Trace your child's hand (with their thumbs together and fingers splayed) onto a piece of paper with a pen. Cut out and paint the bird shape.

Great for:

learning about birds

learning about materials with different textures

1 Cut out a bird shape from the card, and lay it onto a hard surface.

2 Paint the bird, and stick on feathers using glue. Stick on a googly eye. Paint a beak. Turn the bird over and repeat for the other side.

3. Find two sticks in the garden. Tie them together into a cross shape with a piece of string.

4 Pierce a hole through each of the birds with the pencil. Thread the string through the hole and tie it, until all the birds are tied onto the sticks.

Ideas for older children:

From a wider range of materials, such as felt and fabric, look at and feel the different textures, and choose appropriate ones to make different types of birds for the mobile.

Decorated Easter eggs

Easter eggs are special eggs, often given at this celebratory time.
Children will enjoy turning a lowly hard-boiled egg into a beautiful Easter masterpiece. 'Egg-cellent!'

Associated activities:

Chat
Explain that Easter is a Christian festival. Easter eggs are given at this time of the year, as a sign of celebrating new life.

Craft
Put your eggs into a nest by adding shredded brown paper to a coffee filter paper.

Games
Go egg-rolling. Mark a start and finish line. Line the children on the start line on their hands and knees. Using their nose, ask the child to start their egg rolling down the hill. See whose egg gets down to the finish line first.

Have an egg-and-spoon race. Give both your child and yourself (or another child) a hard-boiled egg on a spoon. Have a race against each other. If the egg is dropped, each person carrying the egg must go back to their starting position.

Great for:

learning about Easter traditions

experimenting with patterns

1 *Adult only: Hard boil the egg, by placing an egg in a pan of cold water.*

2 *Adult only: Bring the pan to the boil on a medium heat for ten minutes. Remove the egg from the pan, and allow to cool in an empty egg carton.*

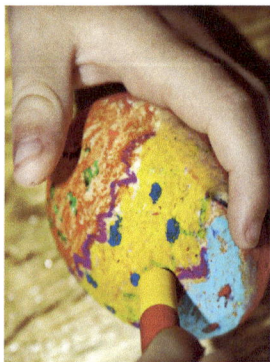

3 Using wax crayons, decorate the hardboiled egg. Think about which colours might compliment each other, and patterns that could be made, for example, zig zags or wavy lines, and swirls.

4 After colouring, leave the egg for half an hour to allow the wax of the crayons to sink into the egg shell.

Ideas for older children:

Use the wax crayons to make repeating symmetrical patterns.

Bunny ears

Traditionally it was said that the Easter bunny delivered decorated Easter eggs to children's houses. Bunny ears are a great activity for Easter time.

What you will need:

White card
Scissors
Glue
Cotton wool
Pink paint and brush

Associated activities:

Act

Put the bunny ears onto your child's head, and ask them to hop around in different directions. Bunnies love eating carrots. Give your little bunny a snack of carrot sticks with a hummus or cream cheese dip.

Game

Hide wrapped mini chocolate eggs around the house or garden. Put the bunny ears on your child, and give them a basket. Ask your child to hunt for the eggs, giving them clues as to the whereabouts of the eggs. This game could also be played with a group of children.

Craft

Make a basket for the hunt. Fold a paper plate in half. Draw on bunny eyes and a nose, stick on a small cotton wool tail, and add a strip of paper into the opening on the curved side of the plate to form the basket handle.

1 Cut out at strip of card, about 6cm wide. Wrap the card around your child's head, leaving a slight overlap, and cut the card. Glue the ends together.

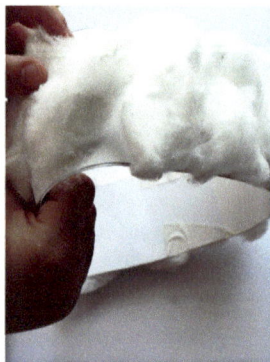

3 Glue small pieces of cotton wool onto the headband.

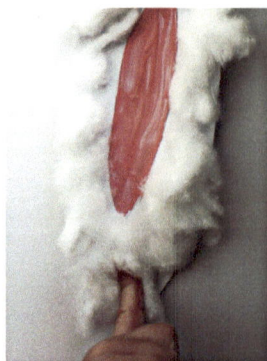

2 Cut out 2 bunny shaped ears from white card. Stick on small pieces of cotton wool with glue. Cut out 2 smaller pieces of card. Paint them pink, and glue them to the centre of the ears.

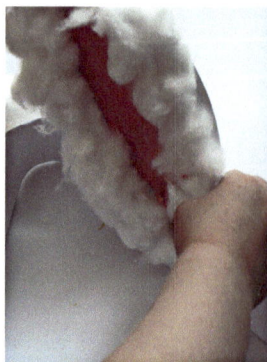

4 Attach the ears onto the head band with glue.

Great for:

learning about Easter traditions
encouraging role-play

Ideas for older children:

Make different animals' ears on top of the band. Ask someone to guess what animal you are.

Chocolate Easter nests

These delicious Easter treats are a great idea to make with children over the Easter holidays. They are so adorable, you may not be able to resist eating them!

What you will need:

For 12 nests:

100g (3.5oz) shredded wheat
200g (7oz) plain chocolate
1½ tbsp golden syrup
50g (2oz) butter
36 mini chocolate eggs

Freezer bag
Mixing bowl
Spoon
Paper cake cases

Associated activities:

Games

Play "Stick the chick in the nest". Draw a nest on a large white piece of card. Cut it out and pin it to the wall. Give each child a piece of paper. Ask them to draw and cut out their own baby chicks. Put a piece of tack on the back of each chick. Blindfold each child in turn and let them see who can put their chick in the nest.

My little girl loves playing "Duck, duck, goose" at playschool. All the children sit in a circle. One child walks behind the others tapping each child on the head saying "duck". However when the child taps a child on the head and says "goose", the "goose" has to get up and chase the first child. If the first child makes it back to the empty spot without being touched, then the second child becomes the new "duck".

Great for:

learning about Easter traditions

developing an interest in baking

1 Crush the shredded wheat in a freezer bag, tied at the end. Put the crushed shredded wheat in a large mixing bowl.

2 *Adult only: Melt chocolate, golden syrup and butter in a bowl over a pan of simmering water.* Add the crushed shredded wheat to the mixing bowl.

3 Use a teaspoon to put the mixture into a paper cake case. Make a well in the centre of each nest.

4 Put three chocolate eggs in the well. Chill in the fridge for half an hour, until set.

Ideas for older children:

Put the nests in a basket, on top of Easter grass or coloured shredded paper. Add little chickens to look after their eggs.

Spring animals

Baby animals often make their appearance in the Springtime. Celebrate this lovely time, by making your own animals. They could be put onto a collage of a green field, and put onto the wall.

White card
Scissors
Cotton wool
Pink, black, red felt
Black pipe cleaners
Yellow, brown, pink tissue paper
Orange card
Glue
Black felt tip pen

Associated activities:

Chat
Spring is the time of year many animals and birds have their young. There is usually a lot more food available, and the weather is warmer. This gives babies time to grow and strengthen before the arrival of Winter.

Trip
Take a walk in your local countryside, and see if you can find a baby lamb being fed by its mother or see a foal finding its feet.

Game
Print off photos of adult animals and their young, from the internet or taken when out on a walk. These could be a horse and a foal; a hen and a chicken; a sheep and a lamb etc. Match the correct adult and young animals together.

Great for:

learning about young animals

exploring nature

experimenting with different textured materials

1 Bunny rabbit: Cut out the shape of a bunny from the card. Glue on small pieces of cotton wool. Cut out and stick on a black eye, a pink nose, and a pink inside of the ear.

2 Duckling: Cut out the shape of a duckling from the card. Glue on scrunched up bits of yellow tissue paper. Add a black tissue paper eye and legs, and make an orange beak from the card.

3 Foal: Cut out the shape of a foal from the card. Glue on a black tissue paper eye, pink tissue paper for the inside of an ear and red tissue paper to make a mouth.

4 Lamb: Cut out the shape of a lamb from the card. Glue on small pieces of cotton wool. Add black pipe cleaner legs. Draw an eye and mouth with a black felt tip pen.

Ideas for older children:

Mr Salad Face

Children will enjoy helping you to prepare this healthy snack.
It's also a fun way to encourage children to eat more salad.

What you will need:

Lettuce
Carrots
Cucumber
Red pepper
Cherry tomatoes
An egg
Two black olives
Cooked sweetcorn
Cress
Chopping board
Childs knife
Cheese grater
A large plate

Associated activities:

Chat

Say that pieces of salad are healthy foods. Draw pictures of different foods, and sort them into healthy and unhealthy foods. Talk about how foods become unhealthy if they contain a lot of sugar, fat, or salt. Too many of these foods can make our teeth bad, and can cause weight gain. It is important to eat healthily and to exercise.

Game

Play 'Salad Bowl'. Children sit in a circle. Each child is given the name of a piece of salad, for example Harry is a tomato, Polly is a cucumber, etc. A child stands in the middle and says the name of two pieces of salad. The children who have been named swop places. If the child in the middle says "salad bowl", everyone swops places.

Great for:

learning about healthy foods

learning about kitchen hygiene and safety

developing awareness of the senses

1 Decide which salad pieces would be good for different parts of the face. Prepare the salad pieces by grating or cutting using a child's knife.

2 Talk about how the different salads smell; feel; what they look like; and taste like. Ask your child, which is their favourite salad ingredient.

3 Arrange lettuce for the face. Add halved eggs and olives for the eyes, and thin strips of olive for the eyelashes. A slice of pepper could be used for the nose, pieces of cucumber for the ears, and tomatoes for the mouth. Add grated carrot for the hair.

4 To make Mr Salad Face's hat, make a triangle shape with the sweetcorn on top of the carrot hair. Scatter cress onto the plate underneath the face for the body.

Ideas for older children:

Make a whole body from salad pieces. Other salads such as celery, spring onions a

Paper plate tiger mask

Paper plates are incredibly versatile, and can be used to make lots of different things. This tiger mask is easy to make, and is a nice introduction to paper plates crafts.

What you will need:

Paper plate
Orange, black and red paint
Paint brushes
White card
Scissors
Glue
Dark coloured pipe cleaners
Pencil
Elastic or string

Associated activities:

Chat

Talk about and make the same noises which jungle animals make. Tigers "raaaaaa", monkeys "ooh ooh", elephants a loud trumpet noise, etc.

Discuss the different foods jungle animals eat. Giraffes eat leaves; monkeys eat bananas, elephants eat peanuts, etc.

Discuss what animals like doing in the jungle. Monkeys enjoy swinging from trees, tigers like to prowl, lions race really fast on all fours, elephants swing their trunks, frogs jump and parrots flap their wings.

Game

Ask your child to pretend to be a jungle animal, imitating the sound the animal makes, the way it eats, and how it moves. Try and guess which animal they are pretending to be. Swop roles, and your child can guess which animal you are.

Great for:

learning about jungle animals

giving animals names

encouraging role-play

1 Paint the paper plate orange. Once the paint has dried, paint black stripes.

2 Cut out and paint shapes from the card: two triangular ears, a nose and a mouth. Glue them onto the paper plate.

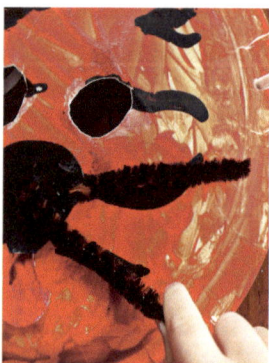

3 Cut out two eye holes. Glue pipe cleaner pieces to the nose of the tiger.

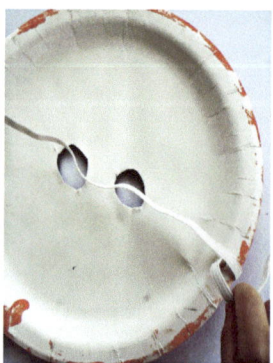

4 Make holes in the sides of the paper plate with a pencil, and thread a piece of elastic or string through, tying a knot at the back.

Ideas for older children:

Make other jungle animal face masks. Add feathers for a bird, fur for a lion's mane, and a trunk for an elephant etc.

Scrapbook

Making a scrapbook with your child is a bonding experience for both of you.
Let your child explain why they want to include particular items into their scrapbook.

What you will need:

A3 card
Paints, sponges, brushes
Decorative bits: stickers,
sequins, fancy paper, photos,
Glue
Coloured sheets of A4 paper
Ribbon or wool
Scissors

Associated activities:

Scrapbook themes:

Holiday
Whilst on holiday, collect
postcards, ticket admission
slips, leaflets, etc. When you
return home, encourage your
child to stick them into their
scrapbook, along with holiday
photos. Ask your child to write
about the best bits of their
holiday, or write in their book
for them.

**Mother's Day, Father's Day,
Birthdays, Anniversaries**
Give a special person a unique
present on his or her special
day. Ask your child to select
special photos, and to tell you
why that photo means
something to them. Write their
quotes in the book.

A book of seasons
Go out on a nature walk, and
collect items along the way.
Use tape or glue to stick them
into the scrapbook.

Great for:

learning about different types
of books

giving a creative stimulus

1 Paint the A3 sheet of card.
When the paint is dry, fold the
card in half.

2 Decorate with stickers, sequins
etc. The child's name could be
written on the front.

3 Slot different coloured sheets of
A4 paper inside the folded card to
make a book. Punch two small
holes in the centre of the folded
edge.

4 Thread a ribbon or piece of
wool through the book, and tie at
the back. Fill the book with
favourite personal items, such as
photos, certificates, ribbons etc.

Ideas for older children:

Write about why items in the scrapbook are important.

my garden

cress
seeds
- p.15

I
grew
a sun-
flower
- p.8

marigold
p.22

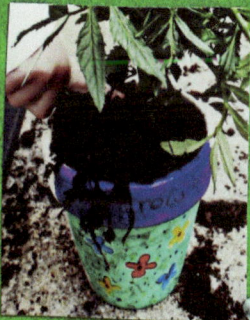

Summer

Summer is the warmest of the four seasons and covers the months of June, July and August.

In the Summer the days are at their longest and the nights are at their shortest. The garden will be full of flowers so make perfume with flower petals or press a special flower that you would like to keep.

Most people spend more time outdoors, playing sports and having barbecues in the summer. Float sponge boats in a paddling pool, collect shells at the beach to thread a shell necklace, and relax with a refreshing fruit smoothie to help cool down.

Butterfly painting

Children love watching beautiful butterflies fluttering in the air. It's a sign that summer has arrived. These butterfly paintings are simple and enjoyable to make, and look fantastic on a garden wall or washing line.

What you will need:

Card or paper
Paints

Associated activities:

Chat

Describe how caterpillars change into butterflies. The adult butterfly lays a tiny egg on a leaf; the caterpillar hatches from the egg and eats lots of leaves. It hangs upside down from a branch, and turns into a chrysalis, from which emerges a beautiful butterfly.

Three of the most common British butterflies are the Red Admiral (dark brown with red bands and white spots near the tips of its wings), Cabbage White (white wings with grey tips), and Peacock (red wings and at each tip a black, blue and yellow 'eye-spot').

Plant

Create an area in the garden that has special plants which attract butterflies. They like purples, yellows and oranges.

Dance

Decorate a sheet, and drape it around your child's shoulders (butterfly wings). Play a quiet piece of music, and ask them to imagine being a butterfly. They could tip toe to the music and flap the sheet (flying), and delicately sit down (landing on a flower), before taking off again.

Great for:

learning about life cycles

developing colour and shape awareness

introducing the idea of symmetry

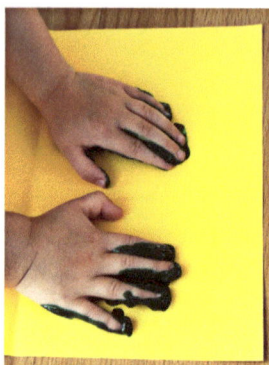

1 Make a fold down the centre of the paper. Press two paint covered hands onto one side of the fold, to make the butterfly wings.

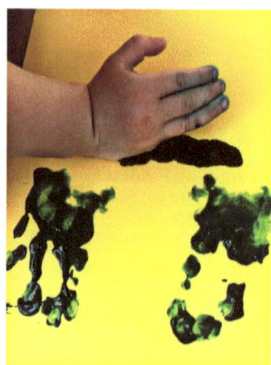

2 Cover the edge of one hand with black paint and press hand along the fold to form the body.

3 Paint the antennae. Add spots to the wings using paint on the fingertips.

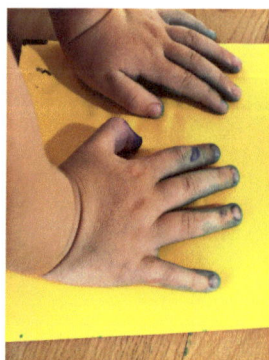

4 Before the paint dries, fold the unpainted half of the butterfly onto the painted side and press down. Open up and cut a butterfly shape around your painting.

Ideas for older children:

Add decoration to the butterfly using buttons, glitter etc. Make sure that one side matches the other. Discuss the idea of symmetry.

Sponge boat

Float these boats in a paddling pool on a hot summer's day, or in the bath tub at anytime of the year. Make boats from different coloured sponges, and with a little push, see which goes the furthest.

What you will need:

Straw
Washing-up sponge
Triangular piece of foam sheet
Glue
Decorative bits, such as foam pieces, stickers etc.

Associated activities:

Chat

Discuss how there are many different types of boats such as sailing, ferries, dinghies, canoes, lifeboats, fishing etc. Show your child photos of boats in books or on the internet.

Role-play

Make a pretend-play boat. Use a laundry basket or decorate a cardboard box to form the main part of the boat. Make a sail by attaching a decorated triangular piece of card to a wrapping paper tube. Tape the sail to the side of the boat. Use cardboard tubes for paddles. Ask your child to pretend that they are on a sailing boat. They can look out for sharks, dolphins, flying fish, seagulls, or other boats. They could bounce up and down a bit over choppy water, or lie back and let the wind carry them along when the sea is calm. They could even take part in a spot of fishing.

Great for:

learning about different types of transport

introducing the idea of floating

experimenting with different textured materials

1 Put a piece of straw through a small washing-up sponge.

2 Decorate a triangular piece of foam sheet with foam pieces or stickers.

3 Attach the foam sheet to the straw mast with glue.

4 Enjoy playing with your boat! Always make sure children are supervised at all times when near water.

Ideas for older children:

Experiment cutting the sponge boats into different shapes. For example, trim one end of the sponge into a V-shape, another into a rounded shape. Which shape makes the sponge boat sail the best?

Fruit smoothie

These healthy fruit smoothies can be enjoyed all year round.
They are easy to make, and a great way of encouraging your child to eat fruit.

What you will need:

Selection of seasonal fruits, such as strawberries, kiwis, grapes, mangos, apples, oranges, bananas.
Child's knife
1 cup yoghurt
½ cup milk
Blender
Spoon
Plastic glass or cup
Kebab stick
Colourful straw

Associated activities:

Chat

Talk about how fruits are healthy foods. Fruit and vegetables contain vitamin C. This vitamin helps the body's defence against infection and helps to keep our bones and teeth healthy.

Games

Cover your child's eyes with a blindfold. Put some fruits into a blender. Once blended, ask your child to taste the drink and guess which fruits you put in. Give them a sticker for each correct fruit.

Play 'The fruit game'. Describe a fruit, such as "It's round, green and crunchy". Ask your child to guess which fruit you are thinking of. The aim of the game is to try and guess the fruit with as few clues as possible.

Great for:

learning about healthy foods

learning about kitchen hygiene and safety

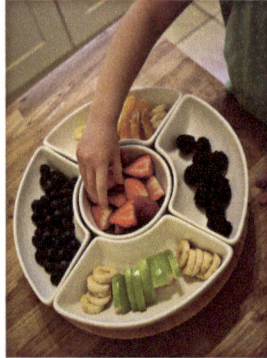

1 From a selection of peeled and cored fruits, taste the fruits, and decide which ones to put into the smoothie.

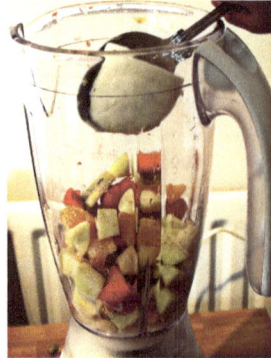

2 Put the favourite fruits into the blender. Add yoghurt and milk. *Adult only: Blend until smooth.*

3 Pour the smoothie into a plastic glass.

4 Choose favourite pieces of fruit and put them onto a kebab stick. Put the stick and a colourful straw into the glass to make the smoothie even more special.

Ideas for older children:

Experiment making smoothies with different fruits.
Talk about which tasted the best, and which ones didn't taste very nice.

Bubble art

Bubbles are great fun to play with, particularly in the summer time.
This art activity has your child creating bubblicious masterpieces with paint.

What you will need:

Bowl
Paints
Washing-up liquid
Spoon
Water
Straw
Paper

Associated activities:

Games
Blow bubbles (without the paint) in the air. Try and pop them before they hit the ground. How many bubbles were popped?

See who can blow the biggest and smallest bubbles. Who can blow the highest and lowest bubbles? Who can blow the most and least bubbles in one go?

Experiment
Blow some bubbles onto a plate. Before they pop, put them into freezer. See the cool results once they have frozen.

Dance
Pretend to be a bubble. Move quickly and slowly to follow the mood of the music. Turn around, float up and down, and "pop".

Great for:

experimenting with different styles of painting

developing colour and shape awareness

encouraging self-expression

1 Mix some paint with the washing-up liquid in a bowl.

2 Add water to the mixture in the bowl, to make it slightly runny.

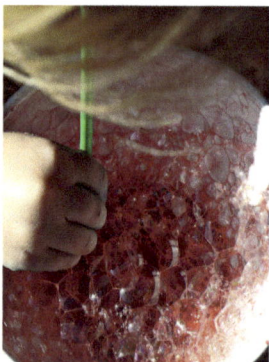

3 Use the straw to blow bubbles in the bowl. It works best if the bubbles spill over the top of the bowl.

4 Place the piece of paper on top of the bowl, allowing time for the bubbles in the bowl to pop. Repeat with different coloured paints.

Ideas for older children:

Put some bubble mixture in a tray. Experiment with different blowing utensils. Which blows the best bubbles?

Perfume

As a child, I loved making perfume from flower petals which I found in the garden.
Your child will enjoy making their own perfumes, using this extremely simple method.

What you will need:

Label
Decorative bits, such as stickers and ribbons etc.
Glue
Fallen rose petals
Bowl of water
Stick
Small plastic container or bottle

Associated activities:

Plant

Sow some flowers seeds in a pot on a window sill. Explain that flowers need plenty of water and sunlight to grow. Easy and fun varieties of flowers to grow include Marigolds, Snapdragons, and Pansies.

Game

Blindfold your child and spray the perfume on your hand. Ask your child to use his or her nose to try to find out where you are. This game can also be played with a small group of children, where one or more of the children are wearing perfume, and the blindfolded child has to find them. Please remember though, that some children may be allergic to perfumes.

Great for:

learning about plants and flowers

investigating the sense of smell

1 Decorate a label with the stickers and ribbons.

2 Go out into the garden and collect 2 handfuls of fallen rose petals.

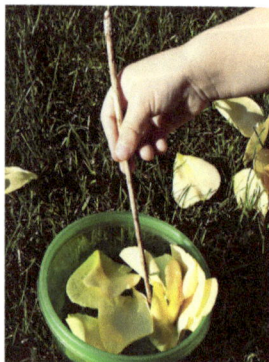

3 Put the petals into a bowl with a little water. Using a stick found in the garden, or a spoon, grind the petals in the bowl.

4 Add the mixture to the plastic container. Give your perfume a name, and stick on the label.

Ideas for older children:

Use other flower petals and leaves to create different perfumes.
Discuss which perfume you prefer.

Teddy Bear biscuits

This is my Mum's recipe. The biscuits are simple to make, and children love to add the ingredients, mix them, and watch them bake in the oven, before eating them. Yum!

What you will need:

For 4 bears:

28g (1oz) caster sugar
56g (2oz) softened butter
85g (3oz) plain flour
(As easy as 1, 2, 3!)
1 tsp milk

Mixing bowl
Hand blender
Rolling pin
Lightly floured board
Teddy Bear biscuit cutter
Cooling tray

For the icing:
28g (1oz) butter
85g (3oz) icing sugar
1½ teaspoon cocoa powder

Associated activities:

Bake

With this same recipe, use a round biscuit cutter to make funny faces.

Sift icing sugar into a bowl, add enough water to make a spreadable paste and then add a few drops of food colouring to get the required face colour.

Spread a teaspoon of icing onto the biscuit and then use edible food decorations to decorate the face, such as sprinkles for the hair. Give the funny face a big nose, rosy cheeks, eyebrows, a curly moustache etc.

Great for:

developing an interest in baking

learning about kitchen hygiene and safety

1 *Adult only: Preheat the oven to 180°c.* Weigh the ingredients and add to a mixing bowl. *Mix the ingredients together with a hand blender.*

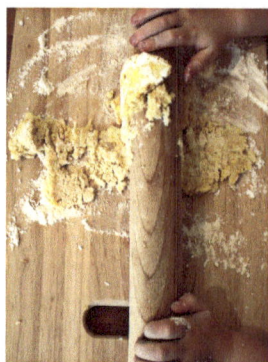

2 Roll the mixture into a ball. Then roll out flat onto a lightly floured surface.

3 Press out a Teddy Bear shape using the biscuit cutter. *Adult only: Put in the oven, on a greaseproof paper tray, for 15 minutes or until the biscuits are a golden brown. Remove from the oven and place on a cooling tray. Leave the bears to cool.*

4 Make butter icing, by mixing icing sugar, butter and a few drops of milk. To make chocolate icing, add cocoa powder. Spread evenly over the bears.

Ideas for older children:

Give the Teddy Bears features, by decorating them with sweets, chocolates,

Play dough garden

Play dough encourages children to think creatively, and to use their hands to shape, and mould. Create a fabulous miniature play dough garden. Who else could live in this habitat?

What you will need:

Yellow, black, red, purple, pink, orange and green play dough
Modelling tools including a plastic knife and rolling pin.
Garlic press
Scissors

Associated activities:

Homemade play dough
Make your own play dough with 1/4 cup salt, 1 cup flour, 1/4 cup water. Mix the flour and salt in a bowl then add water. Knead and squeeze the dough.

Coloured play dough
Divide the play dough into sections, then knead in food colouring.

Glittery play dough
Knead the glitter into the play dough until you get the desired effect.

Smelly play dough
Add spices, teas or oils to give your play dough an interesting aroma.

Textured play dough
Add sand, lentils and other textured materials to create an alternative sensory feel to the play dough.

Great for:

experimenting with modelling techniques

learning about insects

1 Bee: Roll a yellow ball, and press down slightly. Add two black stripes, wings, eyes and a mouth.

2 Snail: Shape a long snake-like piece into a spiral. Leave a little end of the spiral out for the head. Add antennae, eyes, and a mouth.

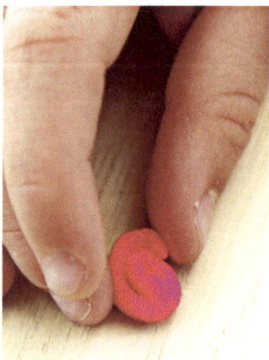

3 Flower: Roll out a thin long snake, and shape it into a spiral. Flatten each layer a little bit. Add leaves and a stalk.

4 Grass: Put some green play dough into a garlic press. Use scissors to cut the play dough to the length of grass that you require.

Ideas for older children:

Older children can use their imagination to create other play dough scenes, such as the sea, space, a zoo, or a play area.

Plant pot

Painting flower pots encourages children to develop an interest in plants and flowers.
They will look great on windowsills in the house, or outside on garden patios.

What you will need:

Small terracotta plant pot
Acrylic paints and brushes
Clear varnish
Soil
Plant or flower seeds
Water

Associated activities:

Plant

The best flowers to grow in pots are: sweet peas, nigellas, poppies, marigolds, and pansies.

Grow sunflowers in your plant pot. Keep a daily diary to record how fast it is growing. The best thing is that they grow really fast!

Craft

Make plant labels to mark where seeds have been planted. These can be made from lollipop sticks or wooden spoons, with the name of the plant written on.

Chat

Talk about the insects you find in your garden, and how they can be beneficial to plants. Worms are good as they make holes in the soil for air and water. Ladybirds are great as they eat greenfly. Slugs, though, eat plants.

Great for:

learning about plants and flowers

exploring nature

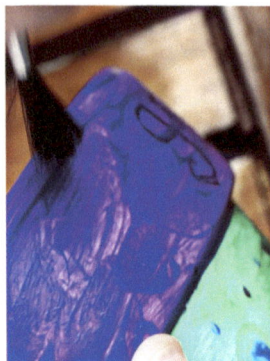

1 Decorate the outside of the pot with the acrylic paints.

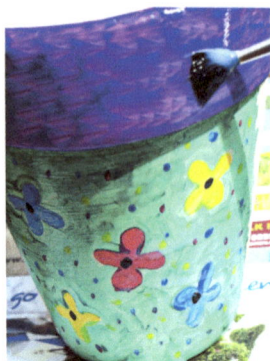

2 *Adult only: Indoor pots are fine to be left at this stage. However for outdoor pots, brush clear varnish over the pot, after the paint has dried.*

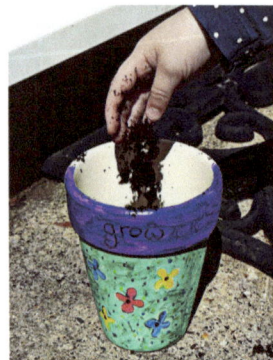

3 Fill the plant pot with soil.

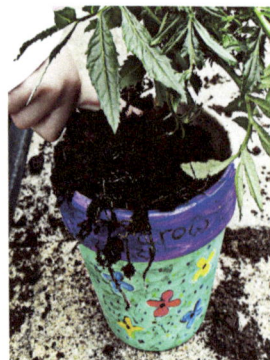

4 Make a hole for the plant (or sow some flower seeds) and cover with soil. Water the plant each day.

Ideas for older children:

Create different effects on your plant pot, by using sponges, or stencils. Paint pictures such as ladybirds or butterflies. Or write the name of the plant or herb, which you are growing in the pot.

Tissue paper flower

Tissue paper flowers look very pretty, and yet are relatively easy to make. Fill a little window box or pot full of these beautiful flowers, they would make a great birthday or Mother's Day present.

What you will need:

Coloured tissue or crepe paper, about 20cm²
A green pipe cleaner

Associated activities:

Art

Tissue paper bleeding: Tear pieces of tissue paper into strips. Flatten the strips down onto a piece card or paper, and using a paint brush, brush water over the top of the tissue paper. Repeat until the card is covered with strips of paper. Then brush over all the strips of tissue paper once more with water. Leave to set overnight. When dried the next day, peel off the strips. The dye from the tissue paper will have run onto the card to mark an arty effect. Great fun to create too!

Tissue paper collage effect: Tear tissue paper in strips. Apply tissue paper to a piece of card. Place the strips evenly for a basic background, or experiment with textures by overlapping the strips, adding small wads of tissue paper, tissue paper stars, wrinkled tissue paper or any other design. Apply glue to the top and repeat with another layer of tissue paper.

Great for:

learning about plants and flowers

developing the skill of folding paper

1 Put 4 pieces of paper together, alternating colours.

2 Fold the tissue paper backwards and forwards, until you have created a concertina of folds.

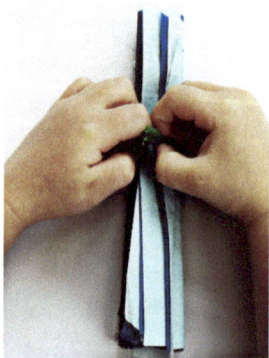

3 Tie the end of a green pipe cleaner around the centre of the tissue paper.

4 Gently open up the tissue paper on each side of the pipe cleaner.

Ideas for older children:

Use more pieces of tissue paper, different sizes and colours to create more elaborate blooms.

Shell necklace

Children love playing on the beach in the summertime.
They will enjoy finding a selection of shells, and making them into a beautiful piece of jewellery.

What you will need:

Shells
Bucket
Water
Drill
String
Scissors

Associated activities:

Games

Order shells in order of size. Put the smallest first in the line, and the largest last.

Find a large shell and put it to your ear. See if you can hear the ocean.

Have a competition to see who can build the most creative sandcastle. This can be done in a sandpit or at the beach. Use shells, seaweed, feathers, stones etc to decorate the castles.

Find a stick or use your fingers to create a picture in the sand.

Have a look in rock pools which are exposed at low tide. See if you can find hermit crabs or sea anemones. Be careful though not to touch them though, as crabs may pinch, and anemones may sting.

Great for:

exploring the seaside

develop an interest in making jewellery

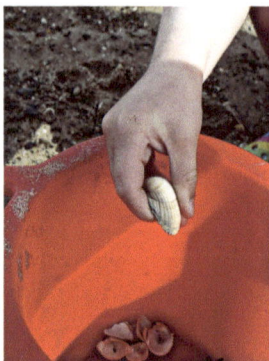

1 Find a collection of shells on a beach, and put them in a bucket.

2 Wash the shells thoroughly with water. *Adult only: Drill a small hole at the top of each shell.*

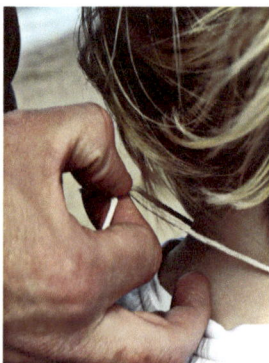

3 Cut a length of string, depending on how long you require the necklace to be.

4 Pull the string through the holes of the shells, and tie a knot above each shell. Continue along the length of the string. Tie the ends of the string together.

Ideas for older children:

Experiment designing different styles of necklaces and bracelets. Add beads and other accessories to make your pieces of jewellery more ornate.

Flower pressing

Children love playing outdoors. They will enjoy looking for pretty flowers, and then by pressing them, be able to keep them, even when the season has ended.

What you will need:

A small handful of pretty flowers
Two pieces of blotting paper
Two heavy books
Tweezers

Associated activities:

Game

Give the child a photo of a flower. Ask them to find that flower in the garden. Can they remember the name?

Craft

Make a daisy chain. Take one daisy and carefully make a small slit with your thumb. Slip the stalk of a second daisy through the slit in the stem of the first daisy. Repeat to make a chain of daisies. When you think your daisy chain is long enough, thread the stem of the last daisy through a small slit at the top of the first stem. Wear it around your neck or wrist.

Food preparing

Make a fruit salad flower. For the stem, cut celery into long strips; segments of oranges and slices of apples and pears can be used for the petals; and the centre of the flower can be made with raisins.

Great for:

learning about plants and flowers

developing an interest in drying and pressing flowers

1 Go into the garden, and collect 4 or 5 pretty flowers, which you would like to press. Talk about why you chose those particular flowers.

2 Put the flowers between two pieces of blotting paper, and put in the centre of a book. Close the book, and put another heavy book on top.

3 Leave for a few days. Open the book carefully, and see if the flowers have dried out.

4 If they have, remove with tweezers. The flowers can then be framed, made into a bookmark with cellophane, or added to a card for a special person.

Ideas for older children:

Draw the flowers that you have pressed, looking carefully at the shape and colour. Talk about the different parts of the flowers, such as the petal, leaf, stem.

Pebble bugs

Pebble bugs are very easy to make. They make great presents, or look great in plant pots or on garden walls.

What you will need:

Four large smooth pebbles
Red, black, yellow, and green acrylic paints and brushes
Eight googly eyes
Black pipe cleaner
White pipe cleaner
Glue

Associated activities:

Chat

Talk about where minibeasts are found. They like moist and warm places, so normally can be found in the soil, under stones and rocks, on the sides of trees or in-between leaves.

Explore

Go into the garden (with a magnifying glass if you have one) and encourage your child to explore, and look around different areas of the garden to find different bugs. Use a trowel or fork to dig in the earth and see what they can find.

Game

Once you have found some minibeasts, say what type they are, for example ladybird or woodlouse. Take photos or draw pictures, and later sort by size. Count features such as legs, wings, etc.

Great for:

learning about minibeasts

identifying features of living things

1 Ladybird: Paint the pebble red and leave to dry. Paint a black face, a black line down the centre, and black spots. Stick on two googly eyes.

2 Bee: Paint the pebble yellow and leave to dry. Paint black stripes across the body. Stick on two googly eyes. Bend two small pieces of white pipe cleaner for wings.

3 Spider: Paint the pebble black and leave to dry. Put four pieces of black pipe cleaner under the pebble, so eight legs are visible. Stick on two googly eyes.

4 Beetle: Paint the pebble green and leave to dry. Paint black stripes across the back. Stick on two googly eyes.

Ideas for older children:

Be imaginative and experiment with an assortment of differently sized and shaped pebbles, stones and twigs, to create other minibeasts: snails, butterflies, moths, caterpillars etc.

Watering can

Gardening is a healthy outdoor activity, which children love to do. Recycle an old milk carton, and make this simple watering can. Children will enjoy helping to water the plants and flowers in your garden.

What you will need:

Empty milk carton
Washing-up liquid and water
Waterproof paints and brush
Stickers
Hammer
Nail
Water

Associated activities:

Games

Water all the red flowers with the watering can. Choose another colour, water all the yellow flowers etc.

Set up several small coloured bowls on the edge of a paddling or swimming pool. Encourage your child to dip the watering can into the pool and and fill up each bowl, as you say the colour. Remember always supervise children near water.

Have a race. This works best if your child has several friends to play. Divide the children into two teams. Give each team a plastic cup and a bucket of water. From the starting line, the first child from each team has to fill their cup with water from the bucket. They then run to their watering can, trying not to spill any water on the way. Next they pour their cup of water into their watering can, before running back to the start line when the next child goes. The first team to fill up their watering can wins.

Great for:

learning that plants and flowers need water and sunlight to grow

1 Empty and clean a milk carton.

2 Paint the carton with the waterproof paints. Add stickers to decorate.

3 *Adult only: Hammer a nail through the lid of the milk carton several times, to make small holes.*

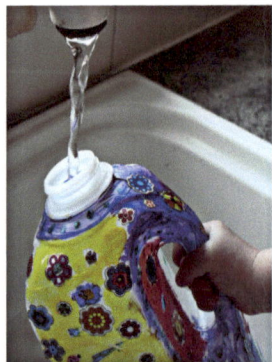

4 Fill the carton with water, and put the lid back on.

Ideas for older children:

Decorate your milk carton so that it looks like an animal, such as a dog or elephant

Autumn

Autumn marks the transition from Summer into Winter, and covers the months of September, October and November.

In Autumn the leaves on the trees are red, orange and brown. Make leaf prints with the fallen leaves. Pine cones, conkers and hedgehogs are other visible signs that Autumn has arrived. A simple pine cone bird feeder could attract all sorts of different birds, or a papier mâché hedgehog is a great autumnal decoration. Halloween and Bonfire Night fall at this time of the year. Celebrate these magical occasions by baking a Halloween pizza, making a pom-pom pumpkin, or by creating an effective firework picture.

Leaf prints

This is a lovely activity for children to do in the Autumn, as leaves have fallen onto the ground. The colours are beautifully rich and vibrant.

What you will need:

Leaves
Bowl of water
Red and orange paints
Paintbrush or sponge
Card or paper

Associated activities:
Art
Make a collage tree out of brown paper. Add the printed leaves to the tree, thinking about the colours that you use if you are making an autumnal tree.

Collect a selection of autumnal leaves on a walk. Take a piece of wax paper large enough to fit several leaves on. Fold in half. Arrange the leaves that you have collected in a pattern between the folds and press the two halves together. (*Adult only: With an iron on low to medium heat, iron the paper until the leaves are sealed.*) Open up the paper and admire the beautifully pressed leaves.

Collect three or four leaves from different trees. Trace the shape of one of the leaves onto a piece of paper. Place the leaves on the table next to the paper. Ask your child to guess which leaf you traced. See if they are right by placing the leaf over the tracing. Repeat for the other leaves.

Great for:

learning about how the changing seasons affect nature

developing printing techniques

1 Collect a variety of different sized leaves.

2 Wash the leaves in the bowl of water, taking care not to damage them.

3 Paint the bottom side of the leaves, where the veins are more prominent.

4 Press the painted side of the leaves down onto the card or paper. Lift up quickly, so that the paint doesn't have time to dry.

Ideas for older children:

Look in a nature book which contains photos of trees and their leaves. Ask your child to see if they can identify which tree the leaves they picked came from.

Portrait picture

This is a fascinating yet simple activity to do with your child. They will enjoy making these self portraits, and you will discover how your child views themselves.

What you will need:

Card
Pencil
Crayons
Scissors
Decorative bits, such as googly eyes, felt, wool, buttons, pipe cleaners etc.
Glue

Associated activities:

Chat

Emotions are feelings, such as happiness, sadness, anger and excitement. We express our feelings by laughing, shouting or crying. Our facial expression is useful, because it shows someone how we are feeling. Ask your child to pull different emotional faces.

Investigate

Look at peoples' faces in magazines or leaflets. Ask your child how they think the people are feeling. What facial expression gives away their feeling?

Game

Draw and cut out several different faces with emotions, for example happy, sad, loving, worried, tired, angry, and surprised. Lay them out on a table. Ask your child a range of scenarios, and ask them to pick a matching emotion card. Scenarios could be: lost a teddy, struggled getting to sleep, eating an ice-cream etc.

Great for:

becoming aware of our own faces and emotions

learning the names of facial features

1 Draw a face shape on the card. Cut it out, and colour in using crayons or paint to match your face colour.

2 Look in the mirror. Point to your eyes, nose, mouth, hair etc.

3 Cut out shapes that look like your features: mouth, nose, eyes, hair etc.

4 Glue on the pieces you have chosen for your eyes, nose, mouth and hair.

Ideas for older children:

Extend the activity by adding additional facial features, such as eyebrows, rosy cheeks, ears etc. Name each feature at the end.

Pine cone bird feeder

This pine cone bird feeder is fun to make, and is a lovely addition to a garden.
Hang on a tree, and watch garden birds come to feed from it.

What you will need:

Pine cone
Hard fat from cooking bacon
Pastry brush
Bird seeds
String
Scissors

Associated activities:

Chat
Talk about what pine cones are. They are pods which carry the seeds of a pine or coniferous tree.

Game
Order the pine cones in size, smallest first and the largest last.

Craft
Make glittery pine cones by rolling a pine cone in glue, and then sprinkle with glitter. See page 102 for instructions on how to make a Christmas tree pine cone.

Art
Use pine cones to create printed artwork. Dip them into paint and press onto paper firmly to create patterns.

Craft
Make a pine cone bird. Bend pipe cleaners into legs and feet; glue on googly eyes for eyes, and glue on a triangular orange foam beak. Make other pine cone animals.

Great for:

exploring nature

learning about animals

1 Go out on a walk and find a pine cone.

2 Smear the fat over the pine cone.

3 Roll the cone in bird seeds so that it is completely covered.

4 Attach a piece of string to the widest part of the pine cone and hang outside from the branch of a tree or bird table.

Ideas for older children:

Look at the birds that come to feed on the bird seed. Record by taking drawings or by taking photos of them, then look them up in a bird book to identify.

Papier mâché hedgehog

Papier mâché is easy to make, and can be used for lots of exciting projects. Children love getting their hands messy in the gloopy paste. This papier mâché hedgehog looks great, wherever your child's work can be admired.

What you will need:

Plain flour
Water
Large bowl
Spoon
Balloon
Newspaper
Pin
Brown, black paints
Paint brushes
Egg carton
Cocktail sticks

Associated activities:

Chat

Read books or watch internet clips about hedgehogs. Talk about how they are nocturnal (they sleep at night), and what they like to eat (insects, snails, frogs and berries). Young hedgehogs are called hoglets or pups. A group of hedgehogs is called a herd. Autumn is a good time to see hedgehogs, as there are plenty of berries and fruit, and they are making sure they have plenty of fat stores to get them through the Winter. They are also out and about considering the best places to build nests.
Hedgehogs normally hibernate between November and mid-March.

Art

Make a handprint hedgehog. Print a light brown fist shape for the head. Using a darker brown paint, make several handprints with fingers spread out and upwards for the spikes. Paint an eye onto the head.

1 To make the paste, add to a bowl 1 part flour and 1 part water, and mix, to a smooth, runny consistency.

2 Inflate a balloon and tie a knot in it. Tear newspaper into strips. Dip the strips of newspaper into the paste and apply to the balloon.

3 Coat the newspaper with more paste, and put on another layer of newspaper strips. Repeat for at least another 3 layers.

4 Leave to dry completely, preferably overnight. Stick a pin through the newspaper to pop the balloon inside.

Papier mâché hedgehog

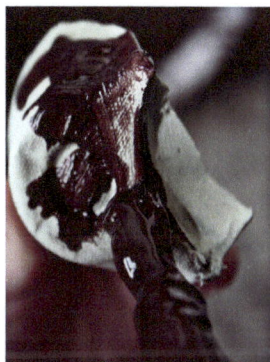

5 Apply brown paint to the newspaper, so that it is completely covered. Paint or stick eyes on the hedgehog.

6 Make the hedgehog's snout, by attaching a painted egg carton section to one end of the hedgehog with tape. Push cocktail sticks through the body of the hedgehog, for the hedgehog's spikes.

Ideas for older children:

Inflate balloons to different sizes to create a whole hedgehog family. Experiment with using different textured materials to cover the balloon, such as paper towels, tissue paper or even cloth.

Rainmaker

Introduce children to the idea of playing a musical instrument, with this easy to make rainmaker. It sounds like rain when it is shaken, and children will enjoy making music while singing their favourite song.

What you will need:

Gravy granule tube and lid
Tissue paper
Tape/glue
Card
Scissors
Uncooked rice
Decorative bits, eg. coloured card, paints and brushes, glitter, sequins etc.

Associated activities:

Chat

Rainmakers are traditional musical instruments originally made and used in South America. They were used to simulate the sound of rainfall, to ask the Gods to let it rain. They are now used in South American festivals.

Playing the rainmaker

Rainmakers teach your child about rhythm. Turn the tube so that the uncooked rice inside falls up and down. This falling motion simulates the sound of rain, as the rice bounces off the sides of the tube. A shaking motion of the rainmaker teaches your child about percussion. Sing a song, whilst shaking the rainmaker.

Game

Cover your child's eyes with a scarf, shake the rainmaker, and see if he or she can find you. Play this game in a wide open space so that they don't bump into anything on their way!

Great for:

learning about new cultures

developing musical skills

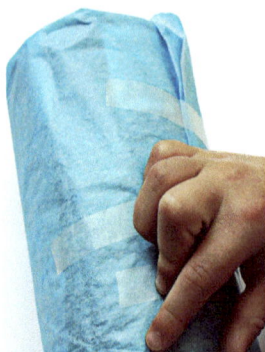

1 Cover a gravy granule tube with tissue paper. Secure with tape or glue.

2 Cut out two circles from the card, to fit the ends of the tube. Seal one end of the tube with one of the pieces of card.

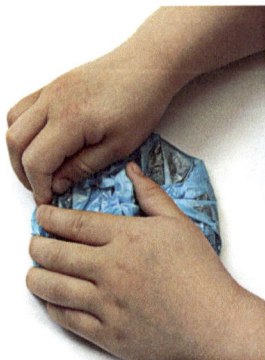

3 Add uncooked rice to the tube, so that it is a three quarters full. Seal the other end of the tube with the other circle.

4 Decorate the tube with strips of card, paints, glitter, sequins etc.

Ideas for older children:

Look at pictures of rainmakers, which are used in South America. These can be foun on the internet or in books. Talk about the bright and unusual patterns.

Flapjack

These oatsome treats are easy to make, and make a great snack or lunchbox addition.

What you will need:

For 10 small slices:

100g (4oz) butter, and extra for greasing
75g (3oz) golden syrup
225g (8oz) porridge oats
30g (1oz) light brown sugar
Wooden spoon
Large mixing bowl
Shallow tin

Associated activities:

Personalise your flapjack
Ask your child which one or two ingredients they would like to add to their flapjack:

75g (3oz) raisins or sultanas
100g (4oz) honey
50g (2oz) dried fruit
A small ripe banana
1tsp ground spice mix
1 apple peeled and chopped
340g (12oz) chocolate chips
Or pour 100g (4oz) melted chocolate on top, and smooth with a spatula. Leave to cool.

Game
Fill several small cups with some of the additional ingredients listed above. Cover your child's eyes with a blindfold, and ask them to taste each pot. Ask if they like the taste? Is it sweet? Is it fruity? Can they guess what the ingredient in each cup is?

Great for:

developing an interest in baking

learning about the melting process

1 *Adult only: Preheat the oven to 180°c.* Introduce the idea of melting to your child. *Melt butter and golden syrup in a pan over a low heat. Leave to cool.*

2 Mix porridge oats and sugar in a large mixing bowl. Stir the melted butter and golden syrup into the bowl.

3 Pour the mixture into a tin, lined with greaseproof paper or greased with a little butter. Press down with a spoon or spatula.

4 *Adult only: Put in the oven for approx 20 minutes, until the mixture is a golden brown colour. Remove from the oven and leave to cool.* Cut into small slices. Store in an airtight container

Ideas for older children:

Show your child how to use kitchen weighing scales. Ask him or her to weigh out the ingredients for baking the flapjacks as accurately as they can.

Sock puppet

These homemade sock puppets are fantastic for stretching imagination.
Your child could make several and host their very own puppet show.

What you will need:

A variety of socks
Decorative bits, eg marker
pens, googly eyes, buttons,
wool, mini pom poms, pipe
cleaners, cotton balls, felt etc
Glue

Associated activities:

Game

The puppet can act as a helper,
who could assist your child with
something that they are
struggling with. This could be
sharing toys, getting dressed,
learning a new song, or doing a
tricky jigsaw. You could say
"Let's ask Clive, and see what
he thinks we should do."

Craft

Make a puppet theatre for your
puppets. Cut the bottom out of
a large cardboard box. Then cut
a large rectangle out of the
front of the box. Paint the box.

Drama

Make a variety of sock puppets
and sitting inside the puppet
theatre, put on a show. Use
different voices for each
puppet.

The puppet(s) could help to
retell a story, encouraging the
child to develop an interest in
storytelling.

Great for:

encouraging role-play

developing creative play

1 Choose a sock from a selection
which you would like to use for
the puppet.

2 Provide a variety of materials to
decorate the puppet.

3 Add googly eyes, and other
decorative bits. Let your creative
juices flow!

4 To make the mouth, tuck in the
tip of the sock (where the toe
usually goes). Cut out a tongue
shape from a piece of felt, and
glue onto to the inside of the
mouth.

Ideas for older children:

Experiment using other materials to make puppets, such as wooden spoons and
gloves. Ask the child which material they prefer making their puppet with and why

Wizard's hat

Play dressing up with this enchanting wizard's hat. Open doors to a magical, spellbound world, where spells are cast and potions made.

What you will need:

Coloured card
String
Pencil
Scissors
Glue
Gold card or paper
Gold glitter

Associated activities:

Craft

A true wizard needs a magic wand. Roll a piece of black card and glue. Put two pieces of white paper at either end, to act as tips of the wand.

Game

Play a magical game, such as hiding jelly beans around the room, and then hunt for the 'magic beans '.

Potion making

Make a magic liquid potion. Fill a plastic cup with a favourite drink. Add a few drops of food colouring, and a decorated straw.

Make a magic 'edible' potion. Put some cold custard in a large bowl. Give your child edible items, such as raisins, cake decorations, and herbs. One ingredient could be added to help them to fly; another to become invisible, etc. give it a stir, and cast a spell.

Great for:

learning about wizardry and magic spells

encouraging role-play

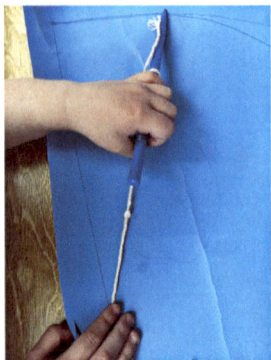

1 Draw a line on the card approximately 15cm long. Hold the end of a piece of string on the halfway point and tie a pencil to string. Draw a semi-circle.

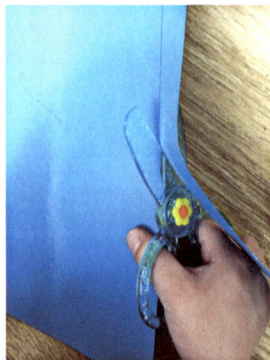

2 Cut out the semi-circle.

3 Make the semi-circle into a cone shape, putting onto a little head to get the correct size. Glue (or *Adult only: staple*) along the seam to keep the hat together. Roll the bottom of the card up, to create a rim.

4 Cut out star and moon shapes from gold paper. Glue the shapes onto the hat. Add glitter to give the hat an extra 'sparkle'.

Ideas for older children:

Ask your child what ingredients they would like to add to a cauldron, such as eye of a newt, frogs legs, witches' finger nails etc. They could then write out a magic spell.

String painting

String paintings are simple, yet look very effective. They are a great alternative to using brushes. Children are fascinated when they see the paints mixing to create new colours.

What you will need:

Paper

Several pieces of string, approximately 30cm long

Paints

Associated activities:

Art

Talk about the colour which is made as two paints mix, and then try it out. Red and yellow make orange; green and red make brown; blue and red make purple; and yellow and blue make green. To make a colour darker, add a small amount of black. To make a colour lighter, add a small amount of white. Warm colours are yellows, reds, and oranges. Cool colours are blues, greens and violets.

A variation on the activity. Before painting, fold the paper in half, make a crease, and unfold. Ask your child to put a paint string on one half of the paper, fold the paper in half on top of the string; pull out the string and open the paper. A symmetrical string painting!

Make more creative paintings using materials, such as tooth brushes and cotton wool to apply the paint.

Great for:

using a different style of painting

experimenting with lines and shapes

1 Dip a length of the string into the paint.

2 Move the string about on the piece of paper.

3 Use a variety of movements such as dragging in circles or making wavy lines, etc.

4 Repeat, using different colours of paint. As the string is dragged across the paper, colours will mix, creating an arty effect.

Ideas for older children:

Experiment with making different patterns with the string, such as holding one end and lifting and lowering in different positions, or 'brushing' the string along the paper.

Halloween pizza

Have a Halloween party with these delicious homemade pizzas. Children will love sharing their creation with family and friends.

What you will need:

300g strong plain flour
220ml water
½ tsp fast action dried yeast
½ tsp sugar
½ tsp salt
½ tbsp olive oil
Tomato puree
Mixed herbs
Grated cheese
Red and green pepper

Mixing bowl
Spoon
Greased baking tray

Associated activities:

Chat

Halloween is a festival celebrated on the 31st October. It is the time when witches, ghosts, etc are supposed to be particularly active.

Bake

Make a ghostly pizza. Follow step 1 and 2 as the Halloween Pizza. Then decorate with slices of mozzarella cut into the shape of ghosts and small bits of olive for eyes.

Crafts

Finger print spiders and pumpkins onto a big sheet of paper or cloth to create a Halloween table cloth.

Carve a Halloween pumpkin. *Adult only: Cut out triangular eyes, a nose and a toothy mouth from a pumpkin.*

Great for:

learning about Halloween traditions

developing an interest in baking

1 *Adult only: Preheat the oven to 200°c.* Mix flour, water, yeast, sugar, salt, and olive oil in a bowl. Knead until the dough is smooth. Place in a warm place for an hour to allow it to prove.

2 Stretch out onto a greased baking tray. Spread tomato puree over the pizza base, and sprinkle with mixed herbs. Cover with grated cheese.

3 Cut up a red pepper into three large triangles for the eyes and nose, and several small triangles for the mouth.

4 Use a slice of green pepper for the pumpkin's stalk and eyebrows. *Adult only: Put in the oven for approx 25 minutes, until the base is a golden brown colour. Remove from the oven and leave to cool.*

Ideas for older children:
Experiment using other toppings for the pumpkin's features. Sweetcorn, pepper, ham, mozzarella cheese and mushrooms work well on pizzas.

Pom-pom pumpkin

Pom-poms look fantastic, and can be used to make lots of different things. Making a pom-pom pumpkin will be a great Halloween achievement for your child, but will need a lot of adult supervision and time breaks!

What you will need:

Cardboard
Scissors
Orange wool (approx 4m)
Glue
Piece of green pipe cleaner
Black felt

Associated activities:

Dressing up

A Halloween cat. Dress up your child in a black leotard, black tights and black plimsolls. To make ears, stick black triangles made out of card to a black hairband. A tail can be made by sewing a black sock (stuffed with another sock) to the back of the leotard. Use a black eyebrow pencil to colour the end of your child's nose and draw whiskers on his or her cheeks. Purr-fect!

Games

This is a Halloween classic. Float several apples in a large bucket filled with warm water. The object of the game is to grab an apple in your mouth without using your hands.

This is spookily fun! Divide an empty cardboard box into several compartments. Cut holes in the sides of the box (big enough to fit a child's hand in, but not to see in). Put cooked cold spaghetti, mashed banana, a satsuma, a damp sponge, and grapes into the inner compartments. Ask your child to put their hands in the holes and try to guess what they are feeling.

1 Cut out two identical circles, about 4cm in diameter. Cut the same sized hole out of the centre of each circle.

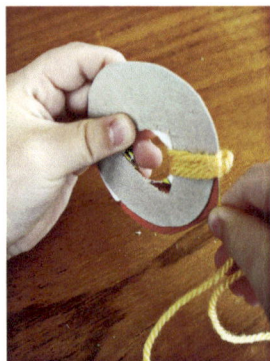

2 Hold the two circles together, and wind the wool through the centre and around the outside of the circles. Keep winding the wool, until the card is covered.

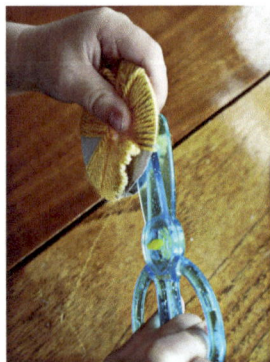

3 Put a blade of your scissors in-between the two pieces of card, cut the wool all the way around.

4 Slide a piece of wool between the two pieces of card, and tie a knot at the centre of the circles. Remove the pieces of card, and fluff out the wool.

Pom-pom pumpkin

5 Glue the green pipe cleaner to the top of the pom-pom.

6 Cut out the black felt into small, triangular shapes, and glue to the pom-pom, making the eyes, nose and mouth.

Ideas for older children:

Use different lengths and colours of wool within the pom-pom.
Different textured materials could be used to add variety.

Firework picture

This is a lovely activity for children in the lead up to fireworks night, a magical occasion filled with excitement.

1 Look at pictures and visual clips of fireworks. Talk about the shapes and beautiful colours, which fireworks make.

2 Draw all over a piece of white card with brightly coloured wax crayons, pressing on firmly.

3 Draw over the picture with a black wax crayon, so that the bright colours are completely covered.

4 Using a cocktail stick or coin, scratch out circles and star shapes, revealing a spectacular firework effect underneath.

Ideas for older children:

Use this same method of crayon etching to produce a big bonfire with people watching around the outside.

Fairy cakes

Start children baking with these easy-to-make and delicious fairy cakes.
They taste great, and are lovely to decorate together.

What you will need:

Makes 12 cakes:

110g (4oz) self-raising flour
110g (4oz) caster sugar
110g (4oz) butter
2 eggs
200g (7oz) icing sugar
A small amount of boiled water
(For chocolate fairy cakes, add
50g (2oz) cocoa powder.)

Mixing bowl
Spoons
Hand blender
Paper cake cases
Sieve
Cake decorations

Associated activities:

Bake
Make a butter cream topping.
Ingredients: 50g (2oz) butter,
85g (3oz) icing sugar, 1tbsp
milk. (Chocolate butter cream:
Add 25g (1oz) cocoa powder.)
Mix the butter, icing sugar, a
teaspoon of milk (and cocoa
powder if required) until
smooth and creamy. Spread
onto cooled fairy cakes.

Decorate
On Valentine's Day decorate
the fairy cakes with hearts. At
Halloween time, decorate them
with spider webs. Holly shaped
icing on the fairy cakes at
Christmas time would make a
fine festive addition.

Craft
Cut out the shape of a fairy
cake from card. Decorate it
with shiny paper, sequins,
glitter, paper flowers etc.

Great for:
learning how to bake and
decorate cakes

1 *Adult only: Preheat the oven to
180°c. Place flour, sugar, butter
and eggs into a big mixing bowl,
and mix with a hand blender until
smooth.*

2 Spoon the mixture into the cake
cases. *Adult only: Bake for about
20 minutes in the oven, until a
golden brown colour. Remove
from the oven, and allow to cool
on a wire rack.*

3 Sift icing sugar into a bowl,
adding a little boiled water at a
time, depending on the thickness
you require. Smooth the icing
over the top of the cakes.

4 Add hundreds and thousands,
chocolate drops, and other cake
decorations to the top of the icing.

Ideas for older children:

Add a few drops of food colouring (pink, blue, yellow etc)
or flavouring (lemon, strawberry, etc) to make different icings.

Winter

Winter is the coldest season of the year. It can be very wet and windy. Sometimes there is also snow, providing plenty of inspiration for a cotton wool snowman. Some animals hibernate, and people enjoy winter sports such as skiing and sledging during the Wintertime.

Winter covers the months of December, January and February. During this time Christmas is celebrated. Bake mince pies to leave for Father Christmas, hang the Christmas tree decoration on a branch of the tree, or make a Christmas cracker to go with your festive dinner. Show someone you care on Valentine's Day by making heart shaped chocolate crispies or by giving a Valentine's heart card.

Cotton wool snowman

Something magical happens when the chill of winter sets in and it snows for the first time. When it's too cold to be outside, children will love making these snowmen indoors. They look great under the Christmas tree, and won't melt when the snow outside does!

What you will need:

Kitchen roll tube
Scrunched up paper
Cotton wool
Glue
Child's sock
Decorative bits: buttons, felt, ribbon
Scissors

Associated activities:

Outdoor fun
Make a snowman outside, when it snows. Remember to wrap up warm! Using your hands, shape snow into a ball. Roll it away from you to collect more snow and grow bigger. Repeat to make a smaller ball for the head. Use extra snow to stick the head on the body. Add large stones or coal for the eyes and buttons; a carrot for the nose; and a stick for the mouth. Give your snowman a hat and scarf!

Games
Say a winter object and your child can pretend to be it. These could include a snowman (tummy forward, arms outstretched to the side); snowball (pretend to be thrown and then curl up in a ball on the floor); or an icicle (stand with arms stretched upwards).

Ask your child to do winter sport actions and you can guess what action they are doing, such as building a snowman, throwing a snowball, skating and skiing.

Great for:

learning about different weather types

1 Fasten scrunched up paper to the top of a kitchen roll tube with glue to make the snowman's head

2 Apply glue to the tube and scrunched up paper. Cover both with small pieces of cotton wool.

3 Tie a knot in the top of a child's sock to make the hat. Cut out eyes, nose, and a mouth from the felt. Use felt or proper buttons for the snowman's buttons.

4 Glue on the felt shapes. Tie ribbon around the neck of your snowman to make his scarf.

Ideas for older children:

Create a painted snowman scene. Paint a snowman onto a piece of blue, grey or black card. Paint a white head and body, hat, scarf, buttons and other facial features. Paint small white paint splodges for falling snow, and a snowy tree.

Bookmarks

Reading books with your child is a lovely way of helping them to learn, and is a great opportunity to have a nice cuddle! Your child will enjoy holding this bookmark while being read to, and putting it in a page of their favourite book.

What you will need:

Card
Scissors
Sheets of felt
Fabric glue

Associated activities:

Make reading fun!
Provide a selection of different books. Talk about which ones they like, and why. Read books about topics that your child is interested in, such as rockets, fairies, horses, cars or bears. Visit your local library, and encourage your child to choose the books that he or she wants to read.

When you are reading to your child, use different voices, and plenty of enthusiasm. Act out the stories, which you read.

Play games such as finding all the princesses in the books, or seeing what colour all the dragons are.

Let your child see you reading. Show them signs when you are driving and tell your child what they say. Show them words on jars of food, magazines etc.

Great for:

developing an enjoyment of reading

learning about shapes

experimenting with different materials

1 Flower: Cut out a rectangular shape from the card. Cover the card with felt, leaving a slight overlap. Use fabric glue to stick the overlapping ends together.

2 Flower: Cut out a flower shape from the felt. Decorate the petals and centre of the flower with more felt pieces then glue to the stem.

3 Shooting star: Cut out a rectangular shape from the card. Cover the card with felt, leaving a slight overlap. Use fabric glue to stick the overlapping ends together.

4 Shooting star: Cut out two star shapes from the felt, one larger than the other. Use fabric glue to stick together. Attach to the felt covered piece of card with fabric glue.

Ideas for older children:

Experiment with using different materials to make bookmarks, such as giant papercl lollipop sticks etc. Which material does your child think makes the best bookmark

INTRODUCTION

...he historic county of Yorkshire, stretching from the river Tees in the north to the river Humber
...nd the borders with Derbyshire, Nottinghamshire and Lincolnshire in the south and from the
...igh Pennine peaks in th... ...n Great Britain and has long been said to cover more acres (3,669,510
...s the biggest ancient co... ...words in the Bible. HV Morton on his motoring tour of England
...t the last count) than ... ... – was of the opinion that it was not so much a county as a
...n the 1920s – *In Sear*... ... e Dales and the North York Moors, and parts
...country: "God's Ow... ...st county in the country.
...women. Co... ... the world: Yorkshire pudding, Yorkshire relish,
of a... ...d sweets), Wensleydale cheese, forced rhubarb and
... And ... ...people throughout history have also made major
Yorkshire te... ... not from No... ...e!), Guy Fawkes, Captain
Harrogate toffe... ...ë sister... ...Judi Dench, Michael
impacts: Eric Bl... ... It is a ... ...d
James Cook, ...the c... ... of ye...
Parkinson, th...
   But it is... ... ap... ...ed by the hand of nat...
landscape, ...thousands of years. The s... ...ty.
or huma... ...to sea level, have resul... ...gerows, with
altitude... ... of ways. The res... ...d farmhouses,
natura... ...and dale, criss-... ...type from
   A ru... ...illsides, and wi... ...ne-built
anc... ...h a medieval par... ...ns and
ha... ...their minster church... ...
a... ...cked into small bays...

...has captured brillian... ...er and
...peaks of Ingleboro... ...oad s... ...he heather-
...d Emley Moors and ... ...east Gill Force and Scalebow
...one pavements of... ...eights of Sutton Bank and the
...vertical cliffs at B... ...e has been equally successful in
...man landscapes w... ...ed with the farming landscapes of
...ales and the Nort... ...ses and their parks and gardens as at
...d or Brodsworth... ...ch as Rievaulx Abbey or York Minster,
...rt innovations s... ...t or the Humber Bridge, the streetscapes
...wns like Richm... ...the grand cityscapes of Bradford, Leeds
...eld. Turn the pa... ...urney through John Potter's *Beautiful Yorkshire*.

...the upper Holme valley, the Digley reservoir overlooks Holmfirth

Mince pies

Mince pies are traditionally served at Christmas time.
Leave one out for Father Christmas on Christmas Eve, and don't forget a carrot for Rudolf!

What you will need:

For 12 mince pies:

350g (12oz) plain flour
225g (8oz) cubed cold butter
2 tbsp caster sugar
½ beaten egg
Pinch of salt
250g (9oz) mincemeat
Milk for glazing
Icing sugar

Mixing bowl
Lightly floured board
Rolling pin
Pastry cutter
Greased bun tin
Teaspoon
Pastry brush
Wire rack

Associated activities:

Chat

Mince pies were thought to symbolise the manger, where Jesus was born. They had a star on top, to represent the Christmas star, which showed the way to Bethlehem. One or two mince pies and a small glass of sherry are traditionally left by the fireplace on Christmas Eve for Father Christmas. A carrot is usually left for Rudolf!

Drama

Act out the story of the nativity with your child. Dress up using towels, adult shirts, scarfs etc. Sing songs such as "Away in a Manger", "Little Donkey" and "Twinkle, Twinkle, Little Star".

Great for:

learning about Christmas traditions

learning baking techniques

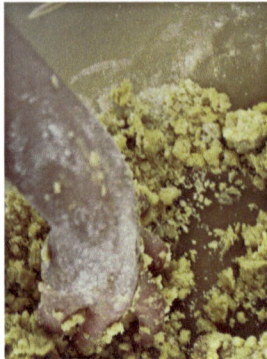

1 *Adult only: Preheat the oven to 200°c.* To make the pastry, rub together the flour, butter and sugar, until it looks like fine breadcrumbs. Add the egg.

2 Knead together the dough mixture. Roll out onto a lightly floured board. Stamp out circles for bases and lids, using a pastry cutter.

3 Put a pastry circle into each lightly greased bun tin section. Add 1 heaped tsp of mincemeat mixture. Brush the rim with milk. Add the lid. Cut a cross into the top of the lid.

4 *Adult only: Place in the oven for 20-25 minutes or until the pastry is golden brown. Leave to cool for five minutes, and then transfer* to a wire rack. Sprinkle with icing sugar.

Ideas for older children:

Make different shaped lids, such as stars, Holly, or Christmas trees.

Christmas tree

Decorating the Christmas tree is an exciting experience for many families. This decorative piece will make a lovely addition to your actual Christmas tree.

What you will need:

Green paint
White and gold card
Glue
Scissors
Sequins
Red and brown paints
Paintbrush
Thin ribbon

Associated activities:

Chat

The traditional Christmas tree is a fir tree. The decorating of the tree is usually a family occasion, where everyone helps. Usually tinsel, baubles and little chocolates are hung on the branches. However children's Christmassy crafts on the tree look fantastic, and really make your tree unique.

Craft

Make a pine cone Christmas tree. Paint the pine cone green. To make it stand upright, put it in a painted egg carton section (the bucket). Dab a small amount of glue, at the tips of the pine cone, and sprinkle on silver glitter and sequins. Give your tree a small bow at the front, and a small golden star at the top.

Great for:

learning about Christmas traditions

developing colour, and shape awareness

1 Press a green paint covered hand several times on a piece of card. Cut the hands out.

2 Glue the cut-out hands together so that the fingers point downwards.

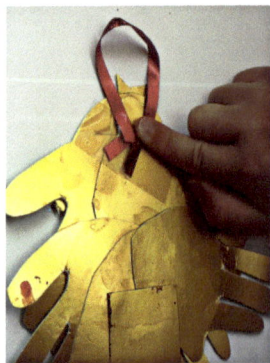

3 Add a gold star. Make a tree trunk from a piece of card, and paint it brown. Make a bucket shape from the card, and paint it red. Decorate the tree with sequins.

4 Attach a loop of thin ribbon to the back of the tree with glue, and hang it on the Christmas tree.

Ideas for older children:

Create a handprint reindeer. Paint a fist shape for the head, and handprints for the antlers. Add googly eyes and a painted red nose.

Christmas cracker

Make your Christmas extra special by giving family members a unique cracker designed by your child. Alternatively use it as a great addition to a Christmas tree.

What you will need:

Two pieces of thick A5 card
Tape
Crepe paper
Glue
Scissors
Decorative bits: festive ribbon, sequins, glitter, stickers

Associated activities:

Chat
Explain that crackers are brightly coloured paper tubes, that when pulled sometimes make a small bang sound. Traditionally a paper hat, small present and joke is found inside the cracker. Crackers are usually pulled just before Christmas dinner is eaten.

Dance
Move around the room, pretending to pull crackers, and when someone shouts bang, do a star jump.

Jokes for the cracker
What goes "oh, oh, oh??
Santa walking backwards.

Where do snowmen go to dance?
A snow ball!

What did Father Christmas say to his wife when he looked out of their kitchen window?
Looks like reindeer.

Great for:

learning about Christmas traditions

experimenting with different textures of paper

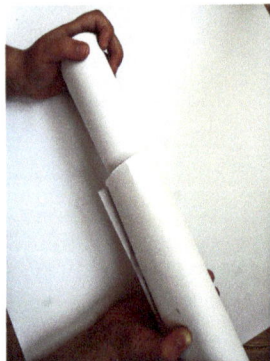

1 Roll a piece of A5 card, overlap the ends and tape together. Roll another piece of A5 card, a bit tighter this time, so it slots snugly into the other roll.

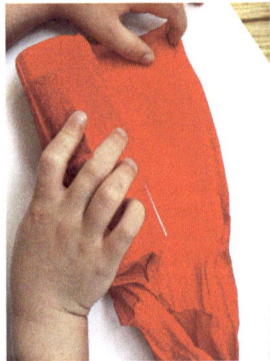

2 Cover each roll with crepe paper (leaving a good length of crepe paper at the end of each roll) and glue.

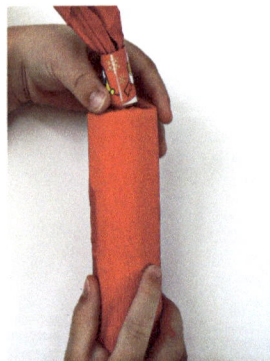

3 Twist the paper at the ends of the cracker, and tie a festive ribbon or wrapping paper around each end.

4 Decorate the crackers with sequins, glitter, stickers etc. Fill as you wish.

Ideas for older children:

Older children may like to write a special message or favourite joke to make cracker even more personal.

Robot head

Make this robot head for your child to wear, and open the door to all kinds of robotic fun!

What you will need:

Cardboard box
Tin foil
Scissors
Kitchen roll tube
Plastic bottle tops
Paints and brushes

Associated activities:

Dressing up

Add a robot style costume to your robot head. Cover a larger box with tin foil. Cut out holes at the sides of the box for the arms. Decorate with an assortment of plastic lids and card cut in a variety of shapes.

Dance

Musical robots: Dance like robots. When the music stops freeze in your robot position.

Games

Pretend to be a robot, walking with stiff arms and legs. Have a race. The first one to reach the finish line, walking like a robot, wins.

Ask your child to pretend to be a robot, and keep walking in a straight line. When they reach an obstacle, they say beep beep beep. That means they need help, so turn them around, and they can keep moving. Make sure that you keep an eye on them, so that they don't hurt themselves.

Great for:

encouraging role-play

developing self-expression

1 Find a cardboard box, that is big enough to go over your child's head. Cover the box with tinfoil.

2 Cut a large square shape in the box and foil, so that your child can see out.

3 Cut an empty kitchen roll in half. Cover each half in tinfoil. Stick these on the sides of the box.

4 Cover two plastic bottle tops with tinfoil, and paint the end. Stick these at the front, and they become lights.

Ideas for older children:

Accessorise your robot head with other metallic adornments such as nuts, bolts, or decorate with buttons or card pieces.

Personalised calendar

A great present for the New Year is a personalised calendar. They are easy to make and children love picking out the required letters for the name in this simple but attractive design.

What you will need:

Stencil letters
Pencil
Card
Scissors
Tack
Different coloured paints
Sponge
Black pen
Stickers
Calendar pad
Ribbon
Glue

Associated activities:

Chat

Talk about the 12 months of the year, and name them. Name the month's that contain your child's birthday, Christmas etc. Explain how there are a different number of days in each month. Sing the rhyme "Thirty days have September, April, June and November. All the rest have 31 except February, which alone has 28 days and 29 in a leap year."

Sort

Sort clothes into summer and winter wardrobes. Discuss whether each item would be suitable for hot or cold weather.

Art

Cut out the first letter of your child's name. Decorate it with paint, sequins, glitter etc.

Great for:

learning about calendars

learning about the days and months of the year

1 Draw around the stencil letters onto the piece of card, and cut them out. Put the letters onto another piece of card, and hold in place with tack.

2 Sponge paint the cut-out letters with different colours making sure you also paint the card around each letter.

3 Before the paint has had time to dry, carefully remove the letters from the card. When the paint has dried, go around each letter with a black pen to make the letter stand out.

4 Add a calendar pad to the bottom of the card. Decorate with stickers. Attach a piece of ribbon to the top of the calendar, so that it can be hung on a wall.

Ideas for older children:

Older children can draw the letters themselves, without the use of a stencil.

uncle ♥ ian ♥

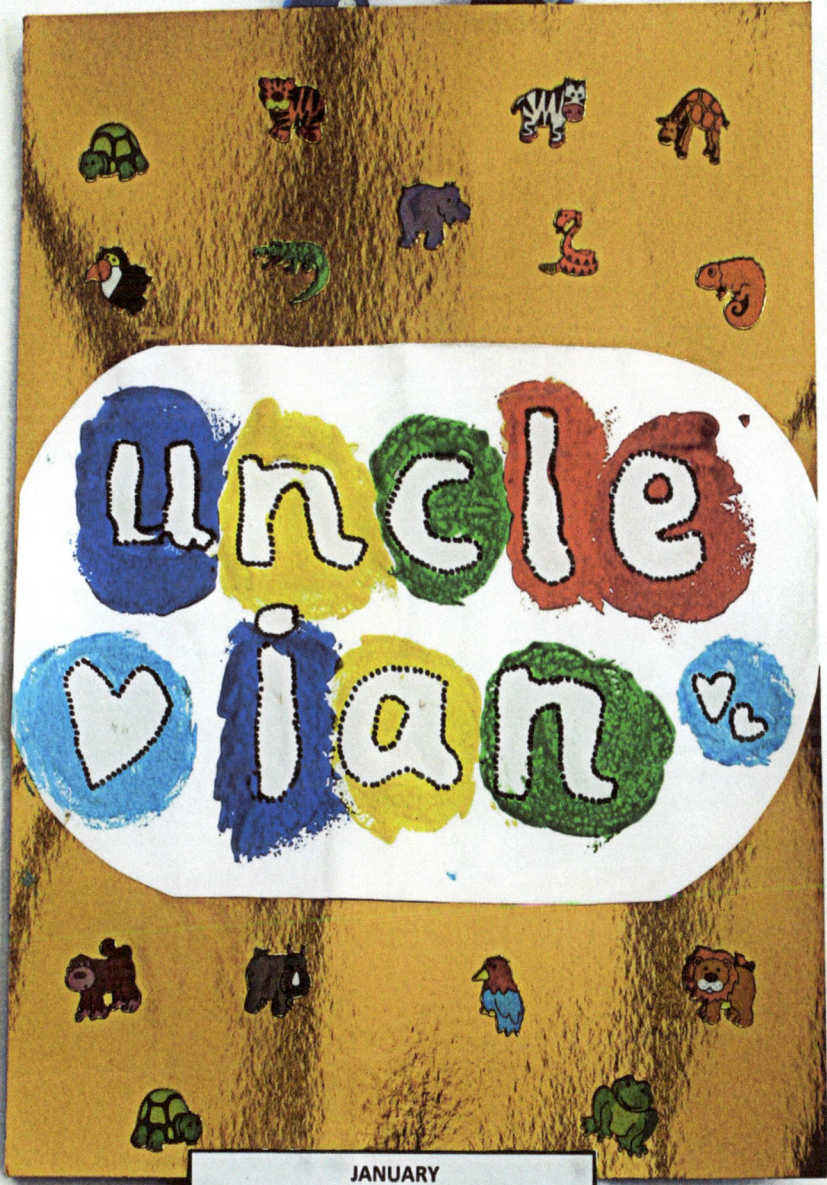

JANUARY						
SUN	MON	TUES	WED	THU	FRI	SAT
1	2	3	4	5	6	7
8	9	10	11	12	13	14
15	16	17	18	19	20	21
22	23	24	25	26	27	28
29	30	31				

Drum

Musical instruments can help children to express themselves, and develop their creativity. Make this homemade drum with your child, and give them a wooden spoon or stick to beat it.

What you will need:

Round coffee drum
Shiny paper
Stickers
Card
Scissors
Glue
Drill
Ribbon

Associated activities:

Rhythm games

Sing a song with your child. Ask them to beat the tune on their drum, and march along in time to the tune.

Sing two well known nursery rhymes with your child. Say that you are going to play one of them on the drum. Can they guess which nursery rhyme was played? When your child guesses the song, it is their turn to play the tune of a rhyme on the drum. Which rhyme is it?

Play a number of steady beats on the drum, ask your child "How many did I play?" Swap roles with your child.

Tap out a simple rhythm on your drum, ask your child to play back the rhythm on the drum. Use long and short beats.

Write a dot on a piece of paper. Your child taps one beat. Next write more beats, again your child taps the beats. Work with your child to come up with symbols for loud, quiet etc.

Great for:

developing musical skills

learning musical vocabulary

1 Cover the container with paper. Decorate it with stickers.

2 Cover the open end with a round piece of card to fit the circle. Hold in place with glue.

3 *Adult only: Drill a hole into each side of the container.*

4 Thread a piece of ribbon through both holes and tie a knot.

Ideas for older children:

Use different materials to cover the open end of the drum, such as fabric. Does produce a louder or quieter sound?

Valentine's heart card

Valentine's Day is a time to show loved ones how special they are to you.
This handprint Valentine's heart could either be framed or made into a card, and will definitely make hearts melt.

What you will need:

Red card
Scissors
Glue
White card
Red tissue paper
Red paint
Sponge
Typed or handwritten message
Stickers
Sweets

Associated activities:

Chat

Talk about Valentine's Day (Saint Valentines Day) being a time when we send cards, flowers and gifts to show someone how much we love them. Traditionally the inside of the card contains a poem, such as "Roses are red, violets are blue, I made this card just for you." Sometimes a question mark is written instead of the sender's name.

Craft and game

Make several heart shapes out of card and decorate so each heart looks completely different. Wrapping paper, paints, sequins etc could be used. Cut the hearts in half. Shuffle the hearts on the floor. Give your child one half, and ask them to find the matching half to make up the whole heart.

Great for:

learning about Valentine's Day traditions

developing an interest in card making

1 Cut out a heart shape from a red piece of card. Glue the heart onto a piece of white card. Apply glue to the red heart and stick on shredded tissue paper.

3 Use the side of a painted sponge to create a border.

2 Put red paint on two little hands. Place the hands onto the card, so that the thumbs and index fingers are just touching the red heart shape. Leave the paint to dry.

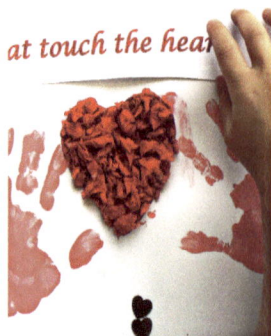

at touch the hear

4 Compose a typed or handwritten message, and stick it onto the card with glue. Personalise the card with stickers and sweets.

Ideas for older children:

Older children can write messages on the card, or stick on a photograph of themselves and the person that they are giving the card to.

Hands that touch the heart

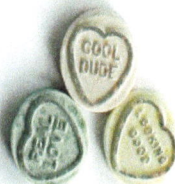

Heart shaped chocolate crispies

Chocolate crispies are very easy and enjoyable to make with children. Add a touch of class to a Valentine Day treat, by putting them in a handmade heart shaped box.

What you will need:

For 12 small chocolate crispies:
220g (8oz) chocolate
120g (4oz) crispies
Measuring jug
Large bowl of boiling water
Spoons and knife
Small heart shaped cutter

Associated activities:

More Valentine treats

Use the pizza recipe on page 86 to make pizza dough. Ask your child to shape the dough into a heart shape, then to roll the edges of the heart inwards to create a pizza crust. Add tomato puree, and shredded mozzarella. Then add other ingredients, which the person you are giving the pizza to, likes.

Cut fruit (strawberries, melon, apples, oranges) into small pieces. Skewer the fruit, onto wooden kebab sticks. Serve with a dipping bowl of melted chocolate.

Make heart shaped biscuits. Use the biscuit recipe on page 50. Instead of using a bear shaped cookie cutter, use a heart shaped one. Decorate the cooked biscuits, with pink writing icing. Write words such as "My Mummy", "love" etc.

Great for:

learning about Valentines traditions

learning about kitchen hygiene and safety

1 Adult only: Melt chocolate in a measuring jug, which is placed in a large bowl of boiling water. Leave to melt.

2 Mix the crispies with the chocolate, so that they are completely covered in the chocolate.

3 Press the chocolate mixture into a heart shaped biscuit cutter. Chill in the fridge for half an hour until nearly firm.

4 Go around the inside edge of the biscuit cutter with a knife, and carefully ease the chocolate heart out.

Ideas for older children:

Experiment decorating the crispies with icing and edible cake decorations.

Cardboard box train

Give your child a selection of old boxes, and empty rolls etc, and see where their imagination takes them. This is one idea of how to make a simple train.

What you will need:

Five cardboard boxes
Paints and brushes/sponges
Card
Scissors
Glue
Other pieces of household packaging
String

Associated activities:

Train games

Take turns being the conductor and taking tickets from the "passengers". Make the sound the train makes, "choo choo", as it chugs along. Encourage acting out activities that might happen when you take a train, such as getting a snack or visiting a new place. The train's conductor could wear a conductor's hat. The other children copy his/her actions, such as blowing an imaginary whistle, waving to bystanders, and chugging their arms.

Hold up a circular piece of card, which is red on one side and green on the other. When the card is green, make a chugging motions with the arms, slowly at first (as if leaving the station), and then gaining speed. When the card is flipped to red, start to slow chugging arms down, until a stop is reached.

Trip

Take a trip on a real train. Let the child take part in buying the ticket. Let them hand the ticket to the conductor. Listen to the whistle, which signals the train is setting off. Enjoy the journey!

1 Put one cardboard box inside another. Paint the cardboard boxes.

2 Paint three more boxes for the carriages, using different colours.

3 Roll up pieces of card and paint black for the wheels. Glue to the side of the train and its carriages.

4 Make two small holes at the back of the train and the front of one of the carriages. Thread string through the holes, and tie the ends together. Repeat to join the carriages together.

Cardboard box train

Great for:

Learning about modes of transport

Experimenting with construction materials

Encouraging role-play

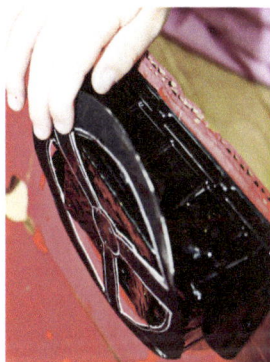

5 Paint a thin cardboard tube and attach to the engine of the train, to make a chimney.

6 Make a steering wheel out of card and other household packaging.

Ideas for older children:

Experiment making other parts of the train with foil, rubber bands, cardboard tubes, old cards, leaves, egg cartons, tissue paper, old holiday brochures etc.

Pasta photo frame

A pasta photo frame can be the perfect gift for a special person in your child's life.

What you will need:

Two pieces of card
Ruler
Scissors
Uncooked pasta in a variety of shapes
Clear, strong glue
Ribbon or string
A favourite photo

Associated activities:

Craft

Make a stand for the back of your frame to display it on a windowsill. Cut out a rectangular shape from thick cardboard. Bend it at one end to make a tab and glue this tab to the back of your picture frame.

Photography

Show your child how to hold the camera. It is best if they hold it close to their face to avoid the camera shaking. Explain that bending down to the subject's eye level can make a better picture.

Take a photograph with your child. Photograph something which they would like to put in the photo frame. This could be a favourite pet, toy, place, etc.

Art

Alternatively add a picture that your child has drawn, possibly of the person that they are giving the frame to.

Great for:

developing an interest in photography

experimenting with different textured materials

1 Measure the photo, which you want to frame. Cut the card so that it is 7cm wider than the photo.

2 Cut a smaller piece of card so that it is 2cm wider than the photo. This is the mount. Use glue to stick onto the larger piece of card.

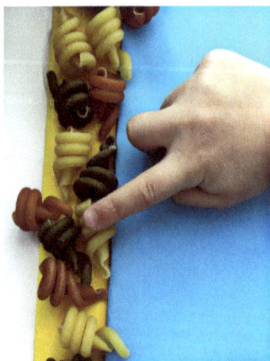

3 Use lots of glue to stick the pasta shapes onto the outer card.

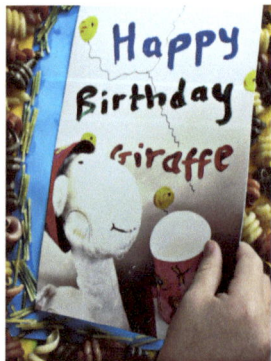

4 Glue the photo onto the frame. Tape a piece of ribbon or string to the back of the frame, so that you can hang your frame onto a wall.

Ideas for older children:

Use repeating patterns with the pasta, or paint the pasta using different colours.

Happy Birthday Giraffe

Jigsaw

Jigsaws are great for encouraging your child to match shapes and colours.
This simple-to-make jigsaw is fun to create and play with afterwards.

What you will need:

Thick card
Paints
Paintbrushes or sponges
Pencil stamps etc
Scissors

Associated activities:

Technique

Jigsaw puzzles can be a great learning tool for children of all ages, as they increase hand-eye coordination. Ask your child to sort through the pieces, organizing them into corner pieces, straight edges or any that have neither. Remind your child to continue looking at the picture on the box, to see which pieces they are looking for.

Crafts

Cut up a copy of a favourite photo into equal pieces. Shuffle the pieces, and put the jigsaw back together again.

Cut up packaging of products, and ask your child to piece them back together again.

Draw a picture (without showing your child) and make it into a jigsaw. Ask your child to complete the jigsaw. You could give them clues and encourage them to predict what they think the objects may be. See if they can guess what the jigsaw is before it's completed.

Great for:

developing logical and spatial awareness

encouraging sorting and matching of colours and shapes

1 Apply paints to different shaped stamps. Decorate the card with the stamps, making beautiful patterns.

2 Divide the card into a number of pieces, by drawing lines. These can be wavy or straight.

3 Using the scissors cut along the lines.

4 Look at the designs on each piece of the jigsaw, and put back together again.

Ideas for older children:

Ask your child to draw a picture and colour it in. Divide the picture into several pieces, and cut it out. Ask friends and family to complete their original puzzle.

Index

Acknowledgements

Ever since I was a little girl growing up in a North Yorkshire village it has been my dream to write a book. I would like to thank a number of people, who have helped to make this possible.

Catherine, my lovely daughter, you have showed so much enthusiasm "I'm excited about what we are making today Mammy", and such patience when we have taken the photographs for each activity. You are a wonderful girl, thank you Poppet!

George, my little boy, you are amazing, fun and have been in my arms for the majority of the activities. Thank you for being you!

My husband Clive, you deserve an extra special thank you for being such a wonderful husband. Your support has been endless.

My Dad, I would never have been able to produce this to the standard that I wanted to without your help. Thank you Mum, you have always been there for me. You are a tower of strength. And to my brother, Ian, for making me laugh.

Phil, Jen, Rich and Jules, thank you for giving me the encouragement to pursue this. We have many laughs, lots of great times and plenty of bubbles!

The Hills, my Aunties, Uncles and cousins (Jenny and Kathleen you gave me the idea!) and the rest of my friends.

Thank you everyone! X

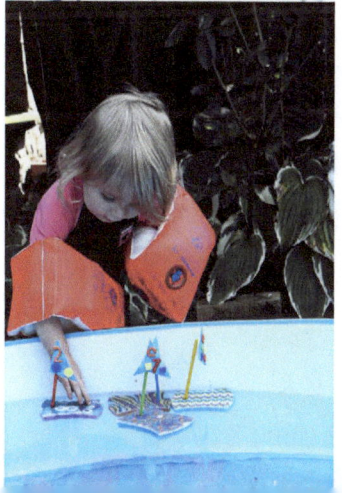

www.ingramcontent.com/pod-product-compliance
Lightning Source LLC
Chambersburg PA
CBHW041305110426
42743CB00037B/2